Foundations for a New Civilization
Structure, Change, & Tendency in Nature & Ourselves

Will Crichton, Ph.D.

Afterword by Carl Semmelroth, Ph.D.

Voluntary Living Press
Kalamazoo Michigan

Foundations for a New Civilization

Structure, Change, & Tendency in Nature & Ourselves

Library of Congress Control Number: 2011937655

Published by Voluntary Living Press
www.voluntarylivingpress.com

For information address:

Voluntary Living Press
3219 Lorraine
Kalamazoo, MI 49008

ISBN: 0-9826232-0-8
ISBN-13: 978-0-9826232-0-6

CONTENTS

ACKNOWLEDGEMENTS

This work has been essentially a solitary undertaking. However, I would like to mention some friends and colleagues who have influenced its content. Many conversations over the years with the late Grant Whatmough have stimulated the interest and motivation behind this work and have been a wholesome reminder of the primacy of fact over construct. Calvin Normore raised valuable objections in the early stages of the work, and his continued interest in it has been encouraging. Kate Kaszuba has asked many probing questions that have made me think about things I might have neglected.

Carl Semmmelroth's intensive interest in this material has been especially encouraging and his questions have led to a number of revisions. James F. Ross, a dear friend of many years, has always supported my work and had some valuable things to say about it. We have independently reached some of the same conclusions on the subject of necessity, but his work on the subject is extensive, while I have only a few observations to make. Finally, I must mention my gratitude to a number of excellent friends whose support is invaluable, and especially to my faithful sister Mary.

PREFACE

This work arose out of a conviction that we could never really understand the humanly important issues (such as ethics) until we understood the fundamentals of reality and nature. In the Twentieth Century, philosophers have considered such an understanding to be beyond the capability of human reason, considering past failures in such projects. However, past failures do not imply the impossibility of success, and it seemed to me that it was time to reopen the topic of elementary ontology.

The right beginning is half the project, and I was fortunate in focussing on the ancient debate over the continuity or discreteness of change. How one comes down on this issue seemed to me to determine the character of one's thinking on all topics. It eventually became evident that the argument was based on the premise that there are changes, structures, and real tendencies.

After a number of years of pursuing the argument and correcting mistakes, my initial conviction seems to have been confirmed. The argument has yielded elementary principles that apply with the same immediacy at all levels of scale or organization. Consequently, they yield insights into issues such as health, ethics, and culture that are as close to the elementary principles as are the implications for physics.

1 A NEW UNDERSTANDING OF NATURE

We need a new way of understanding nature. The old ways, based on supernaturalism, are insupportable and no longer command belief. The way of modern science is powerful and wonderfully informative in some ways, but it is one-sidedly focused on material and mechanistic aspects of nature.

We need a new way of understanding nature, because our civilization based on supernaturalism and science is winding down. This civilization, which began about the time of Plato, some 2500 years ago, was born out of disillusionment with the polytheisms of the early city-states. In those religions the gods were not thought of as remote from human beings but as readily accessible and an available source of advice, mainly through dreams. But during the first millennium BCE, educated persons began to face the fact that the gods were not literally real. And if that were so, they were left without that source of advice.

This had the effect of throwing people on their own mental resources. This was not a comfortable position, since it is obvious that much of what we need to know is not available to us through ordinary means.

The effect of this was to pose a problem — how to know what to do, *or* how to know how to find out what we need to know in order to know what to do.

Thus, around 500 BCE new ideologies arose in China, India, Persia, Palestine, and Greece — problem-oriented ideologies centered on the general problem just stated. In the West this led to Western philosophy, theology, and science, all devoted to solving problems.

A problem-oriented Culture

1

There is no doubt that this problem-oriented attitude has resulted in very great intellectual productivity and the actual solution of many problems. However, there is, we might say, a problem about the problem-oriented culture. **A problem is a particular puzzle to be solved — a question. The custom of beginning with a question focuses attention on particular features of a situation, singled out from reality or experience in general. Solving the problem is answering the question about that particular combination of features and translating that answer into practice. Modern science and technology have made a fine art of this.**

But the key to success in solving problems is the exclusion of other considerations from the puzzle. And that exclusion results in systematic ignorance as to the effects of implementing the solution **other than** those accounted for in the problem and the solution — the notorious side effects.

Thus we get the effect that has often been noted: solving a problem generates other problems. In recent times we have often seen that the conditions produced by the solutions to

Problem solving is treating some feature of experience in isolation.

problems are more serious than the problems that were solved. And often they are of a sort that cannot readily be formulated as other problems. Consequently, we substitute for those unformulable "problems" more manageable problems of a more restricted and focused sort, thinking that in solving them we may "solve the problem", that is, remove the harm that resulted from solving the first problem. This, however, is not a likely outcome

Creating more problems than you solve.

for the same reason, namely that the side effects are unknown until they appear.

For these reasons I say that our culture of the last 2500 years has run its course and cannot continue much longer, is indeed crumbling bit by bit. When solving problems generates more problems than it solves, problem solving has become unworkable.

But is there any other way? The key to this question is the distinction between **attitudes** and **policies**. Policies are like problems: they are focused on particular features of reality or experience — do this

Is there any other way?

under these conditions. And policies result from solving problems, whereas **attitudes result from a way of understanding the world and particular situations.**

Attitudes have more effect than policies. Policies are psychologically shallow — oriented to particular situations. Attitudes, at least those that result from a general conception of the world and of human life, are psychologically deep. They govern the broad character of behaviour. When deep attitudes are inconsistent

Attitudes have more effect than policies.

with policies, the attitudes determine behaviour in ways that subvert the policies. Imagine a government that has a policy of encouraging and facilitating small business; but suppose that the politicians forming that government conceive their best personal interests as lying in associating with the rich and powerful. They may intend to facilitate small business, but their actual measures are likely to be such as to facilitate big business and make life more burdensome for small businesses.

Many people are concerned about the environment and mean to be acting so that they are not contributing to its unsustainability. But their desire for the luxurious life of the middle class in wealthy countries is greater than their desire for a sustainable environment; consequently, they continue to contribute to its unsustainabilitiy. Attitudes have more effect than policies.

A culture of the best attitudes

What will replace our dying culture of the last 2500 years? What will the new phase of Western culture, or world culture, be? We must either build a new one or see governance deteriorate into the rule of warlords and brigands. I propose replacing the preoccupation with problems and their solutions with a preoccupation with cultivating the best attitudes. (This does not mean that we would never concern ourselves with solving problems, but that solving problems would not be the central preoccupation of the culture.)

And how are we to know what the best attitudes are? If attitudes result from an understanding of the world, the most adequate attitudes may be expected to result from the deepest and truest understanding of the world.

And that is why I say we need a new way of understanding nature.

2 THE PRESENT WORK IN RELATION TO MODERN SCIENCE

It is important to say that this account of nature does not compete with science, as we know it. It offers a deeper foundation than the commonly accepted foundations offered by physics, but not such as to be inconsistent with the well-established results of physics, as far as I can tell. It cannot do what conventional science can do. Science is measurement-based; this account is not. Much of modern science is observational, but theoretical science is based on hypotheses that are then tested against observations. When close agreement is found the hypotheses are accepted as true. This is legitimate and has yielded insights into nature that are among our greatest achievements. However, it is a special kind of understanding of nature, not an understanding of what is **found** in the world but an understanding in terms of **questions put** to the world. The questions are ours, not nature's. The theories are models rather than descriptions.

The present account is based on a different method, not the indirect method of hypothesis and verification but the method of deduction from premises drawn from experience — very general premises, namely that there are changes, structures, and tendencies. This may not seem a very promising approach, but persistence yields a great deal more than one would expect or than I did expect. The results may be said to have been **found** rather than **constructed**, though of course the arguments had to be constructed — certainly many of them are different from what I would have anticipated.

Modern science has two seemingly alien but closely related motives: on the one hand to know what the real constitution of the world is, and on the other hand to harness that knowledge technologically. Science has found out a good deal about the constitution of the world, and that knowledge in itself does not determine the kind of technology one will develop. One may wish to know the laws of thermodynamics and also think that heat engines are a curse rather than a blessing. It is not that knowledge that makes heat engines attractive. But if one's **underlying** conception of reality is purely material, excluding transcendence, then one's sense of what is useful to humanity will be shaped by that conception, and heat engines will appear to be obviously beneficial, their pollution, noise, and general ugliness seeming comparatively insignificant. I am not arguing for the elimination of heat engines, but pointing out that the kind of knowledge of the world that modern science provides is not really an understanding of the elementary nature of reality, though it is often thought to be so. It does not govern attitudes, but the materialist conception of reality that has historically accompanied and largely shaped modern science does govern attitudes.

The present investigation of nature, then, is aimed at the sort of knowledge of elementary principles that will shape one's general attitudes and one's conception of what a good life is. That knowledge, far from being in any sort of conflict with modern science, will collaborate with it to determine the kind of technology to be based on it.

3 THE PRESENT ACCOUNT OF NATURE: A PREVIEW OF SOME IMPORTANT FEATURES

Things in the Past Are Real:
In this account of nature, changes take place in temporal space — four-dimensional space in which changes are ordered along the temporal dimension ("space-time" in physics). The future has not yet happened; the past has already happened. Thus, the boundary between past and future is the end of the results of change, and beyond that there is only empty space. Behind that, in the past, there is structure, the result of changes. Thus, changes extend structures in space, and structural elements farther out came into existence later.

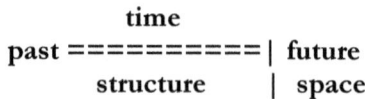

```
                      time
          past ==========| future
              structure  |  space
```

If changes extend structures in space, the past portions of those structures are still there in temporal space, not in the present of temporal space, however, not here and now, but in the past of temporal space, which is a place in four-dimensional space. Thus, nothing ever goes out of existence but only recedes into the past portion of temporal space. The past is real.

Change is extension of structure.

This is true of the properties of structures as well as of structures. Consider that a change in the properties of a thing brings something new into

6

existence and removes something from existence. Within the changing present moment, this is what happens. But in reality altogether, a change in the properties of a structure extends the structure with a new property, while the preceding property recedes into the past. It does not go out of existence.

The past is real.

If material processes exist in the past after they have terminated, the same is true of human beings. When we die, we cease to live, but we do not cease to exist. We exist in the past, and it is our complete life that exists in the past exactly as it was lived, and will exist throughout all time. **Death is not annihilation. Nor is our existence after death a disembodied one.** We continue to exist just as we were, as bodies with relationships, only the process of our lives is

Death is not annihilation.

at a standstill, because the body has ceased to function. To appreciate the full significance of this we need to look at another important feature of this account of nature.

Causality by Patterns:

According to this account, the principle of causality is that what happens tends to be similar to existing patterns. More exactly, structures tend to be extended in ways that are similar to existing patterns. This is limited by what is possible. A structure, when extended, is necessarily similar to what it was before being extended, since only the new portion is what is added on. So, if you consider the various potential extensions of a structure, those that are more similar to existing patterns are more likely to occur.

I argue that this is the only possible principle of causality. To give an idea of how that can be argued, here are the crucial steps in the argument.[1]

1. There must be a creative factor that creates the events; otherwise tendencies would not be real.
2. What, then, gives the creative factor a bias towards certain events? It can only be what is in the category of structure and change, since the bias has structural properties, and there are no structural properties outside that category.
3. What is in the category of structure and past changes is inert. The only way in which it can bias the creative factor is by being what it is, in other words, by providing the patterns that events might resemble

---

[1] I do not offer this as a proof. For that see Appendix A, "Causality by Patterns".

An important point about this is that similarity does not depend on distance. Consequently, patterns are just as effective if they are in the remote past or in remote parts of the universe as they are if they are nearby.

Some of the existing patterns are more prevalent than others, and a potential extension of a structure that is similar to a more prevalent pattern will be more probable than one that is similar to a less prevalent pattern, given the same degree of similarity. So the principle of causality may be summarized by this formula:

Tendency due to pattern =
similarity to pattern x prevalence of pattern.

Everything in the past is available
as a direct cause, a pattern:

- ☐ Thus, a person may be formed by patterns found anywhere in the past of the universe.

- ☐ The more similar the person's potentialities are to given patterns the more fully those patterns will probably be incorporated into the person's nature. (Thus, persons as wholes may have certain strong affinities to past persons as wholes, giving rise to the notion of reincarnation.

We are shaped by patterns from the past.

- ☐ The other side of the same coin is this: that we will always be patterns for any future lives that may resemble us to a significant degree. Our potential influence goes beyond our lifetime and will exist for all time.

We are patterns for shaping future lives, and will always be.

Transcendence:

Reality is not confined to space and time. Underlying causality by patterns is a transcendent factor that compares the patterns with the potentialities and creates the events as biased by the tendencies. I call this factor the **creative factor**, since it creates the changes in structure in response to the universe as it exists already. In its creative relation to the material universe it may be called God. But far from being the human-like god of tradition, it is only the creative factor of nature. The creative factor is not in space or time, not in the categories of structure and change, and therefore has no structural properties, therefore no purposes, intentions, or preconceptions of the universe.

The creative factor's response to the material universe is the original and perfect paradigm of consciousness. The creative factor is unable to respond to the universe other than exactly as it is. It can neither select its information, nor add to it, nor process it, since these would presuppose structure and change outside the category of structure and change. Its response is immediate, since there is no medium through which it could pass and no transcendent

The creative factor is conscious of the universe.

process that could delay it. And it is transparent, since only the universe as it is and a creative response to it can be the content of it. If *we* were able to respond to the entire universe immediately and transparently, we would say we were conscious of it. By the same criterion we must say that the creative factor is conscious of it.

The creative factor's consciousness of the universe opens the way to taking account of the full spectrum of human experience. The first principle of science is that experience takes precedence over theory. When experience clearly contradicts theory (emphasizing "clearly"), experience must be accepted and theory revised. This principle does not permit us to be selective as to which modes of experience are to take precedence over theory, although, to be sure, the interpretation of experience is often problematic. During the age of modern science, materialism (the view that all reality is in space and time) came to be accepted as self-evidently true by a prestigious segment of society and acquired the status of orthodoxy, so that the precedence of experience over theory has been habitually compromised (as it was earlier by the orthodoxy of religious doctrines). I wish to restore experience to its rightful and (in principle) acknowledged place.

It has generally been supposed that the only alternative to materialism is supernaturalism, the view that there is a higher realm of being outside of space and time with a nature of its own, with intentions and intelligence and the ability to override the natural causality of the material world, or that is the author of that causality. The argument here presents a third alternative — a transcendent being that has no nature of its own but is the creative agency of the nature of the material world — a nature that is defined by material conditions.

Methodologically, traditional theology founded its conclusions in the concept of God as the primary reality, known by revelation. The conclusions drawn here are founded in the logical necessities of structure, change, and tendency, known to be real by common experience.

The Necessary Patterns:

A number of properties of structures, changes, and tendencies can be shown to be necessary since the conceptual alternatives to them involve contradictions. That being the case, wherever structures, changes or tendencies occur, they will have those properties. These necessary properties are patterns for analogous properties.[2]

For example, that nothing goes out of existence is a necessary pattern. Analogous to it is the repetitiveness of a process in temporal space (the continuation of a pattern in temporal space), which in commonplace terms is the endurance of a thing over a period of

Necessity, the core of nature

time (in other words, it continues very much the same through its changes, as a house or a tree does). **The necessary patterns constitute the permanent core of nature, since they are both universal and unchanging.**

The most important of all analogues of necessary patterns is **individuality**, which is the analogue of the discreteness of change and structure (that changes occur in minimal discrete steps and structures are composed of minimal particles). A study of the necessary patterns and their analogues shows that the maximization of individuality, both individually and as the

Individuality, the dominant tendency of nature

total individuality in a region of the universe, is the dominant tendency of nature. Individuality consists of two properties: wholeness and distinctiveness. Wholeness is the property of being a single thing, or of being more like a minimal change or particle than a multiplicity. Distinctiveness is the property of being in contrast with surrounding things.

To understand wholeness we need to bring in the principle of complementation.[3] The body of a particle is not the entire particle; the entire particle includes the structural relations (the spatial relations) of that body. In other words, the particle is an element of structure, not merely a member of a

---

[2]They cannot be patterns for the properties identical to themselves, since those properties occur by necessity and therefore cannot be affected by tendencies.

[3]See Appendix A, "8. Structural Complementation".

set of particles. When we generalize this to individual processes, what they are is defined by their individuality, which is subject to degrees. Thus, the statement for individual processes is that an individual process includes **those external relationships of its body that combine with the body to make it a whole process**. For example, a human body increases in wholeness as it acquires personal relationships, business relationships, geographical relationships (where they live, their home, their habits of movement, and the like), and so on.

Thus, the tendency for total individuality to be maximized leads, on the one hand, to differentiation, as distinctive individualities emerge, and on the other hand, to integration, as complementation relates different individualities as components of larger individualities. For example, the human body is organized as parts within parts in complementation with one another to constitute a functional whole.

Individuality is both qualitative and quantitative. Qualitatively, it is what a thing is, what makes it that particular thing — my individuality is what I am. Quantitatively, something can have individuality to a greater or less degree. What I am can be more or less clearly defined, more or less highly developed, more or less clearly distinguished from other individualities.

Individuality is not simple singleness and separateness, like the discreteness it is analogous to. It is the wholeness and distinctiveness of organized systems. In the important cases of individuality, wholeness is the integrity of a functional structure or organization. The effective functioning of a system requires that it be integrated, in other words that it have wholeness. And it must be a system distinct from other things. A function (such as the function of the heart to pump blood) is a process in temporal space. The function (pumping blood) goes from the system that performs the function to the system that benefits from the function (from the heart to the cells). For this to happen there have to be those two systems (which

Functionality is individuality serving individuality.

may be one and the same). They have to be definite systems, that is, they have to have wholeness and distinctiveness. And the function that goes from one to the other has to be a definite process in temporal space, that is, it has to have wholeness and distinctiveness.

The benefit of a function is a contribution to the individuality of the system that receives it — a function maintains or improves what a system is, maintains or enhances its wholeness and/or its distinctiveness. We hear about dysfunctional families. What that means is that the family fails to do what is needed to keep it together, to keep it from dissipating into its environment — in short, to maintain its wholeness and distinctiveness.

Considering the role of individuality in functionality, we can see that living things have far more individuality than any other systems. This is **total individuality**, adding up the individualities of all their functional subsystems and functional external relationships.

Health:

Individuality is the relevant concept for analysing health. Health implies that all subsystems are functioning so as to maintain the individuality of the whole system. And health is really the health of the entire person, not merely the body but the body with its external relationships, those that make up the individuality of the person as a whole. Health is functional individuality, individuality of the body, and individuality of the person. But health is more than that; these constitute the **capability** of living fully. But health is not only the capability but also the **actuality** of living fully. It is primarily living fully, and that presupposes having the capability of doing so.

A Foundation:

These features of the present account of nature provide a foundation for giving an intelligible account of human consciousness and its various manifestations — choice; reasoning; objectivity and distortion; truthfulness, evasion, and falsification; ethics and self-validation, happiness and the best attitudes.

4 THE KEY TO A NEW UNDERSTANDING OF NATURE
(THE ELEMENTS)

How do you begin to develop a deeper understanding of nature than that which science has already given us? You need a notion of the **elements** of reality. Physics gives us a notion of the elements as being the **elementary particles**. But reality is more than **things**; it is also events or changes, and also the underlying causes of these.

Elements must be both irreducible and comprehensive, and they must together comprise all of reality. This implies that they cover both the parts and the whole, as well as intermediate wholes and how all these work together.

I propose that **structure, change** and **tendency** are genuine elements of reality, at least some of them. Structure and change are material, but tendency, although affecting material things, may not be entirely material; it may have an ingredient that transcends time and space.

To treat these as elements of reality, we must understand them in a general way. A structure consists of things separated and connected by something real. Things arranged in space constitute a structure; they are separated and connected by space.

Structure, Change, & Tendency

Anything that happens to a structure is a change.

Tendency is what defines the probabilities of the next possible changes or events.

Understood in this way, these categories are very general. There are some who are sceptical about all ontological concepts, but if one is not sceptical about the existence of things separated and connected by space, that they undergo events, and that events are affected by tendencies, then I think one will see that the category of space and time is characterized by structure, change, and tendency. I argue that there is also an entity not in space and time without which there would be no real tendencies. But I begin with just structure, change, and tendency.

I am not proposing that these are the only categories with which one can understand reality, only that they are especially powerful ones that permit deductive reasoning to be carried to surprising lengths.

There are two levels of reasoning in this account of nature and of our nature. The argument for the foundations (Appendix A and the identification of necessary patterns in Appendix B) is, as far as I can see, rigorously deductive. The account of the analogues of the necessary patterns, of the importance of individuality, of ethics and self-validation, and of culture is less rigorous and depends as well on empirical observations.

5 WHY IS THIS IMPORTANT?

Structure, change, and tendency are not only present in all levels of scale and organization but are exemplified in all of them as well. Not only does a human community have structures in it, but it is itself a structure. Changes are the same kind of thing whether they happen to molecules or human bodies or international relations. Tendencies are the same kind of thing whether they are the tendencies of molecules or of

Applicable directly at all scales and levels of organization

human bodies or of international relations. Thus, holistic and mechanistic causality are brought under the same principles, principles that not only apply at all levels but bring all levels together under these same principles. And there is no gulf between the topics of physics and chemistry and those of psychology and ethics, but all are just variant applications of the same principles.

The **necessary** properties of these elements (the alternatives being contradictory) constitute the core of nature — the necessities of nature. When the argument is followed through persistently, one discovers a considerable list of these

Necessities of nature

necessary properties of structure, change, and tendency.

Then when these necessities of nature are applied to the analysis of humanly important topics such as ethics, we see, for example, that ethical standards are not only necessary foundations for a viable community but are also rooted in patterns in the foundations of nature in general.

6 TENDENCIES VS. LAWS

Part of the legacy of personified monotheism is the concept of laws of nature. Modern science in its early phases was seen as an effort to find out the laws God had decreed for the universe.

By now, for most scientists, the idea of God has dropped out of the picture, but laws remain the central concept of the form that the principles of nature take.

Nature seems to be like a game; the rules = laws.

This conception of nature is equivalent to that of a game. A game is defined by rules. Some rules specify what the board or the playing field is to be (space-time). Others specify the pieces (elementary particles). Others specify the actions: what is permitted and what is prohibited (laws of nature). Still others specify the consequences of the actions (also laws of nature).

Nature differs from a game in that the rules of nature are not given. We are players in this game, but we play it without having been given the rules. It is like playing a computer game, where the computer enforces the rules without telling us what they are.

Science is playing to find out the rules.

This analogy between a game and nature is not lost on scientists, who sometimes think of themselves as metaphorically playing against God, tricking God to reveal the rules.

This conception of nature is deeply ingrained in Western culture, to the degree that it seems self-evident, and is taken for granted. That was certainly my experience in my reflections leading to the present project.

But consider this: Can there be rules if no one has formulated the rules or undertaken to play by them? If we leave a personal God out of the picture, what becomes of the laws of nature? If we think of the universe in materialistic terms, what are the laws? They are not things in the universe, made of some kind of particles. They are not statements written down, or in the minds of scientists, at least such statements could not be fundamental principles of nature, since they have no authority over the universe.

Laws presuppose an intelligent deity.

So I say the conception of nature on the analogy of a game presupposes a deity as traditionally conceived, an intelligent being who can formulate laws and "play" the universe in accordance with them.

Modern science, therefore, preserves a vestige of supernaturalism. It was a major move towards naturalism, but is still only partway there. A genuine naturalism will not attribute events to an agent that acts on transcendent principles. Laws therefore can be useful models, but they cannot be among the fundamental principles of a genuine naturalism.

Tendencies can be naturalistic.

It took me some time to digest these thoughts, and in the process I began thinking in terms of tendencies rather than laws. Whereas no place can be found in the material world for laws (just as the rules of a game are not inherent in the board and the pieces but only in the players), tendencies are naturally thought of as inherent in material processes. The argument shows that they are both that and also transcendent.[4]

---

[4]See Appendix A, 3. Transcendence.

7 TRANSCENDENCE[5]

There is a creative factor that is not in space or time and is thus devoid of structure or change. This creative factor bridges the gap between cause and effect by creating the events in response to what is in temporal space, that is, to the state of structure and its history of changes. That state of structure and its history of changes define what the tendencies are. By bridging the gap between cause and effect the creative factor makes the tendencies efficacious.

There is only one such creative factor responding in that way to the entire universe, and there is only one universe.[6]

Is it God or Energy?

The proof that there is a creative factor (briefly, that changing structures would not define efficacious tendencies without it) also tells us what its properties are, or rather, its relations to the material world, namely: it connects causes to their effects so as to make tendencies real & effective. If nothing connected causes and their effects, tendencies would not be real, since they could have no effect.

The creative factor produces the effects,

thus connecting causes to effects.

---

[5]See Appendix A, 3. Transcendence.
[6]See Appendix A, 4. One Creative Factor and One Universe.

The creative factor has no specific tendencies of its own, because **specific** tendencies specify probable states of structure, and the creative factor has no structure of its own, therefore, no possible states of structure to be specified.

To make tendencies effective, it must produce the changes as biased by the tendencies. Tendencies exist **before** the changes for which they are causes. Therefore, if the creative factor did not produce the changes, the tendencies would be disconnected from their effects.

Thus, the creative factor responds to the material universe by producing new changes, as biased by the tendencies it finds specified there.

Where does this creative factor fit into familiar conceptions? The answer is that it fits between the cracks, so to speak. There have been various conceptions of a deity, but I think they all represent God either as the **author** of the universe and nature or as a personal or quasi-personal being that gives the universe reassuring qualities **over and above those provided by nature**. The creative factor does not do any of these things, but it has other properties that perhaps are reassuring on a more rational basis.

☐ The creative factor has no characteristics that presuppose having structure. Therefore, it is not a person in the sense of being intelligent, having purposes, and having intentions. It has none of these properties in itself, but this does not rule out having them in its relations with the material universe.

Not a personal god.

☐ The creative factor has no specific tendencies of its own.

☐ For these reasons, the creative factor is not God as conceived in traditional religions — not a personal God of the sort that we can communicate with in the way that we do with one another. But it has other personal characteristics. And it is the creative source of everything in the material world. And God has not always been conceived as a personal being, so that the creative factor could be called God, or an aspect of God. But what better deserves the name "God" is the creative factor in its responsive and creative relationship with the material world.

Is the creative factor energy?

☐ Energy is located in space and time and is a quantity of potential action.

☐ The creative factor is not in space and time.

Not energy

☐ The creative factor takes the potentialities for action from what is in space and time. Therefore, it is not itself a quantity of potential action.

What is it? It is the transcendent active element of nature, that creates all events as biassed by natural tendencies. Nature in the full sense has an active and a passive component (the creative factor and the patterns in the material world), which may be called God and nature respectively.

But Is There a Real God, Then?

The notion of a **literal person** who is the benevolent and omnipotent ruler of the universe must strike thinking persons as rather ludicrous, as well as insulting to the victims of all sorts of horrors. (By a "literal person" I mean a glorified version of a human being). Just as thinking persons in the first millennium BCE could no longer accept the old theologies as literally true, so thinking persons in our time have more and more been unable to accept the personified versions of monotheism as literally true. The creative factor is in no sense the ruler of the universe. However, although not literally a person, the creative factor **in relation to the universe** is **analogous** to a person in that the creative factor can be thought of as the will of the universe and the universe as its body, so the will of the universe is exercised over its body in response to the tendencies of that body. This may seem to justify thinking of God as ruler of the universe. But it is misleading, since it seems to imply that God's actions are intentional and that the workings of nature have transcendent intentions behind them. This leads one to see misfortunes as injustices and to ask such questions as "Why did this happen to me?" or "What did I do to deserve this?" or "Why didn't God prevent this from happening?" Jews have agonized over such questions in view of the Nazi holocaust, and many of them have rejected God as a result.

In monotheistic theology there are trends that have little of the personal about them, such as the Christian idea that God is to be identified with Being, Truth, and Goodness.

In the present approach to understanding reality there is no room for a literally personal conception of a deity. The creative factor in itself is devoid not only of intentions but also of structure and specific tendencies. But the creative factor's relationship to the universe gives the creative factor structure and tendencies, namely those of the material world. And the attributes of God as so conceived (the relationships that make up the creative factor's relationship to the universe) are not so very different from Being, Truth, and Goodness.

These relationships are:

☐ **Creation**, which is the creative factor's creation of the universe particle-by-particle.

☐ **Truth**, which is the creative factor's inability to respond to the universe otherwise than exactly as it is, with no omissions, alterations, or distortions.

☐ **Beneficence** is the tendency of nature to maximize total individuality. Unlike other tendencies, it is based on very special and elementary patterns. Individuality is the analogue of the necessary patterns Particles and Discreteness. Particles are the product of minimal acts of the creative factor, and discreteness is the relationship between successive minimal acts and their products. Beneficence is the product of the creative factor's comparison of the potentialities of individual processes with these necessary patterns. Whereas Truth is the creative factor's "seeing" of things exactly as they are, Beneficence is the creative factor's "seeing" of Particles and Discreteness in the potentialities of individual processes — potentialities for individuality. Thus, Beneficence is the product of the elementary products of Creation and Truth. As such it can reasonably be regarded as one of the relationships that constitute God. Of these, Creation comes first, since particles and discreteness are properties of what has been created. Truth comes next, emerging with the existence of created entities. And Beneficence comes later, after individual processes have come into existence.

☐ Rootedness, by which the creative factor relates processes to patterns, giving them tendencies. For a living process its relationship to the creative factor as Rootedness constitutes its soul.

☐ Influence, by which the creative factor relates processes as patterns to potentialities (their own and those of other processes), giving them causal efficacy. For a living process its relationship to the creative factor as Influence constitutes its spirit.

Of these five transcendent relationships, I would suggest that Creation, Truth, and Beneficence constitute God, while Rootedness and Influence (soul and spirit) are the aspects of a person that are directly mediated by God.

The meaning of "sacred", I think, is "pre-eminently important and not to be tampered with". These transcendent relationships are pre-eminently important, since they underlie the deepest and most important aspects of ourselves. And they are beyond being tampered with. However, our conceptions of them can be tampered with. We can but ought not distort our conceptions of them or regard them as unreal in order to relieve ourselves of responsibility. This is to say that the transcendent relationships are sacred. And individuality, as the predominant tendency of nature and the pre-eminently important thing about ourselves, should also be regarded as sacred.

God and Nature:

The creative factor is, on the one hand, God as related to the universe through the transcendent relationships, and on the other hand, the active element of nature as realizing tendencies. God and nature are the two poles of the one polarity — nature as the inert source of the patterns that define tendencies, and God as the active component making these tendencies real in actual events.

8 SOME SPECIAL NECESSARY PATTERNS[7]

The necessary patterns are the core of nature

Discreteness, Particles, etc.:

I have already commented on individuality as the analogue of Discreteness.[8] Then, most of the necessary patterns that I list in Appendix B have analogues in support of individuality or that presuppose individuality. Individuality is thus the central theme of this account of nature.

The Transcendent Relationships:

The transcendent relationships Creation, Truth, Rootedness, and Influence are necessary patterns. Beneficence is not a necessary pattern but the most elementary tendency of nature.

Creation:

The fact that every extension of structure is created by the creative factor — Creation — has generosity as an analogue. The creative factor's creation of extensions of structure has no ulterior motives and is unconditional and perpetual. The sort of person that almost everyone spontaneously likes and is drawn to is the sort who has an analogous attitude to life — an unconditional impulse to enhance life (that is, individuality), both in substance and as perceived — to emphasize the vitality and vivacity of others and to do their bit towards enhancing it. And there is this about individuality: the wish to enhance it precludes any wish to invade and manipulate it, because this would violate the very notion of individuality. Generosity is not the impulse to give

---

[7] See Appendix A, 10. The Necessary Patterns, and Appendix B.

[8] See The Present Account of Nature, A Preview: The Necessary Patterns.

away all that one has, but the impulse to encourage, feed, and protect the individualities of other lives.

Truth:

The creative factor's inability to respond to the universe otherwise than exactly as it is, with no omissions, additions, or modifications is the original paradigm of truth. It is this paradigm of truth and truthfulness (seeing things just as they are and acting according to things just as they are) that affects people's conscience when they think of telling or not telling the truth. Other variations of truth may be philosophically problematic, but this simple and primary one is not.

Rootedness:

This refers to the rootedness of ongoing processes in the past and in the necessary patterns throughout the universe. Although Western culture has studiously ignored this relationship (both in physics and in human nature), most of the cultures and religions of the world have given it a central place (especially with respect to one's ancestors), either as something treasured or as something feared.

Rootedness is complementation by similarity with patterns. This is an aspect of what one is, of one's individuality. Far from being an evanescent series of fleeting present moments, out of nothingness into nothingness, as some notions would imply, what one is is a permanent and growing structure in temporal space, interrelated with other such structures and anchored by causal roots to all parts of the universe present and past.

Influence:

Influence is the inverse of Rootedness, that is, the rootedness of potentialities in the given process. The potentialities may be its own, or they may be those of any other similar process (later in time). In human terms, the potentialities are potentialities for one's own actions or thoughts, or they may be the potentialities of another person similar to oneself in relevant respects (we are patterns influencing the conduct and development of others).

Taking account of all these modes of complementation gives us a sense of the dimensions of a complete person and that a complete person is much more than just an animal body. And Rootedness and Influence extend what one is to the entire universe, including its entire past and potential future, through relations of similarity. Similarity is a relation that is mediated by the creative factor and as such is not a relation within temporal space but transcending it. However, like structural relations it links one to things in other places. These relations of similarity may be called **para-structural**, and a complete person may be thought of as a para-structure reaching throughout the universe and its past. The structural process of the body and its contemporary relationships grows out of that para-structure. And just as individuality is subject to degrees, so is being a para-structure. The para-structural relations with other individual processes exist to the degree of their similarity.

An important case of rootedness is one's complementation by similarity to other persons as patterns. This is an essential element in the dynamics of a moral community. To be a member of a community is to be unable to ignore or be altogether uninfluenced by the examples set by others. And this also implies that others are unable to be altogether uninfluenced by the example set by oneself. This is one important way in which we are responsible for others.

Supersession (The Passage of Time):

Another major necessary pattern that is of great importance for personal relationships is **Supersession**. This necessary pattern consists of the succession of sets of active tendencies (which define the "living" present), each set being superseded by a new set. This is the passage of time, which replaces things in the present time with new things in new present times.

The analogues of this necessary pattern include very diverse relations between living things from a moral perspective. The creation of an extension of structure replaces one set of potentialities and tendencies with another. Thus, its analogues include all sorts of patterns of sacrifice. These include predation and consumption of food — sacrificing other living things for one's own sustenance, which is the replacement of other lives with one's own; the succession of generations (one generation dying so that another can take its place in the world and in society); as well as self-sacrifice (parents depriving themselves of conveniences, pleasures, and even necessities in order to serve the needs of their children).

The difference between sacrificing another for oneself and sacrificing oneself for another is morally as great as possible, but the forms of the patterns differ only by being converses of each other, and they are alike in being the sacrifice of one living thing for the preservation of another. I am not suggesting that predation is morally wrong; it is if the victim is of one's own moral community. The point is that these opposites are rooted in the same elementary facet of nature.

It is good to know what sorts of behaviour have a powerful foundation in nature and what sorts are only oddities. People tend to think that what they see as morally wrong is unnatural, and that the doers of such deeds are human freaks and therefore the more to be condemned. The necessary pattern Supersession shows us that both morally admirable deeds and morally revolting ones such as predation on one's neighbours have a powerful foundation in nature. This should not lead us to excuse atrocities, rather to understand that we need to design education so that moral character will be equal to following the good analogues of necessary patterns and avoiding the wicked.

The lesson coming from finding out what the actual tendencies of nature are is not that we are victims of nature and cannot help doing the wicked things that we may be inclined to do. On the contrary, it is that we need to cultivate the good tendencies that our **volitional** nature is capable of (volition is also based on nature) so as to be **selective** in following original nature. We cannot escape from original nature. But causality is always selective. In any minimal event, only one among the many potentialities for that event is realized. It is by no means the case that to follow nature is to do every sort of thing that is according to nature. Nature only prescribes tendencies, not events. God is selective in creating events, and we must be selective in our contribution to the creation of events.

9 THE DIMENSIONS OF TIME[9]

Perhaps this is as good a place as any to summarize the nature of time according to this account of nature.

Time has three aspects: a sequence of events, a sequence of extensions of the structure of the universe, and a series of extensions of a local process. We may call these **elementary time**, **spatial time**, and **local time**.

Elementary time:

Elementary time is just a sequence of minimal events.[10] A minimal event consists of a state of the material universe and the coming into existence of a new particle, making a new state. Between the coming into existence of one particle and the coming into existence of another particle is the time of the state resulting from the creation of the first of these particles. That time is **a time** but not a duration of time. Duration is defined by the number of steps of elementary time that are covered. This is the implication of the discreteness of change and therefore of elementary time.

This is a difficult idea for most of us to grasp, because our conscious experience presents time and change as continuous. Because we do not perceive the fine grain of structure or change, these appear to vision and touch to be continuous. But the first lesson that the critical examination of the nature of things should have taught us is that things are not always as they appear to the senses. The senses do show us something of reality, and something of the greatest importance to ourselves, namely things as they

---

[9]See Appendix A for the demonstration of the results summarized in this chapter.

[10]See "Discreteness & Individuality" and Appendix A, " 2. The Discreteness of Change & Structure".

relate to us and as we respond to them. These are not mere "appearances" but features of the world as it really is. However, to get at the underlying elementary realities, we need to rely on logical reasoning rather than simply our conscious experience.

Before the first particle was created, the creative factor existed[11]. Therefore there was a time before the material world existed. But it makes no sense to ask how long that time was. Just as the time between the creations of two successive particles has no duration, so the time before the first particle's creation had no duration. It was **a time** but not **a stretch of time**. Periods of time are defined by numbers of minimal events. This means that if we knew how many minimal events occurred in one second, we could assign the corresponding fraction of a second as the "duration" of a minimal event. But it is an extension of a measurement to a case where it does not really apply. The scale of minimal events is so minute relative to events on the scale of ordinary life that, for ordinary purposes, change is virtually continuous and therefore should be treated as continuous. But to extend this to our understanding of minimal events is fallacious.

Sequential time:

This is the sequence of particles in the order of their creation. It is also the sequence of complete structures of the universe, each identical to its predecessor except for the inclusion of one more particle. Whereas elementary time is pure time, sequential time is its material product.

Spatial time:

This is the direction in temporal space of earlier and later creations. This is a dimension of space, and space is continuous[12], so that spatial time **is continuous**. But the discreteness of elementary time is reflected in the discreteness of structure. That is, what is **in** temporal space is discrete, although temporal space itself is continuous.

Local time:

The time of local processes is time in the most familiar and commonplace sense. This is the local portion of spatial time.

When these different applications of the concept of time are sorted out, we get a coherent and demystified conception of time. What is common to these "dimensions" of time is the relation of before and after, past and future, of what has happened and what has not happened.

Motion & Rest:

---

[11]See "One Creative Factor & One Universe".
[12]See Appendix A, "7. Empty Space Is Continuous".

An enduring individual thing is really a process. It is always being extended into the future until it terminates. In ordinary thought we distinguish motion from rest, but this distinction has reference, not to **temporal** space, but only to the space of the present. In reality, a process that is "at rest" is moving (growing) in the direction of local time. A process that is "in motion" is moving both in the direction of local time and also laterally to the direction of local time, that is, at an angle to the direction of local time.

In another sense, a process is "at rest" at each time between occurrences of new particles, that is, nothing is happening. In this sense, Zeno of Elea argued that a moving thing is always at rest.[13]

---

[13]See discussion of Zeno and Aristotle in Appendix A.

10 INDIVIDUALITY

Individuality is the principal analogue of the discreteness of change and structure (separateness of minimal parts, themselves being strictly single with no distinction of parts).

Individuality of persons is a matter of great importance to all of us. Individuality has two aspects: distinctiveness, or contrast with neighbouring things (it is important to us not to be a "carbon copy" of anyone else but a distinctive individual), and wholeness, or being like a single thing rather than a multiplicity (a person who is "falling apart" is losing their wholeness or integrity). But individuality has much wider importance than its importance for persons. A comprehensive list of the necessary patterns and their analogues shows that the dominant tendency of nature

Individuality, the dominant tendency of nature

is the maximization of individuality, both in individual processes and in the universe generally. This tendency underlies the way the universe is structured into individual processes from the smallest to the largest (nuclei of atoms, atoms, molecules, cells, organs, living bodies, stars, solar systems, galaxies, groups of galaxies).

Individuality = wholeness & distinctiveness.

31

Individuality (wholeness and distinctiveness) is not only the dominant tendency of nature. It is also the foundation of the difference between good and bad, desirable and undesirable.

To get some sense of this connection, you have to consider how individuality figures in functionality. For something to perform a definite function it has to be an integrated structure or system, such as a hammer or a clock or a heart — this is wholeness or unity. Such an entity must also be a distinctive thing, something that stands out among other things (the way the blood vessels do among other parts of the body) — the definiteness of the function presupposes the distinctiveness of the functioning entity.

External & internal relationships essential to individuality

Functionality presupposes individuality.

Individuality is on the one hand **what a thing is** — its unique makeup that makes it individually distinctive and whole — **its being**. On the other hand individuality is a **quantity** — something can be more or less distinctive, can gain or lose distinctiveness (its boundaries can be penetrated, for example), and it can be more or less whole and can gain or lose wholeness (eating a meal improves blood sugar level, restoring the functional integrity or wholeness of the body). Individuality as a quantity is a criterion of evaluation — a work of art is said to lack unity, a person is said to be falling apart, an orchestra is said not to be together — this is wholeness as a criterion of functionality and value.

Individuality is both quantitative and qualitative.

Complex Systems:

To understand the role of individuality in complex systems such as animals, it is necessary to think of their relationships. Relationships are not something added on to the system; rather, they contribute to its individuality and therefore belong to what it is. What you are as a person includes your interactions with your environment, your affiliations, your dependencies, and your responsibilities. This is the principle of complementation — the

relationships of a system complement its body as features of its individuality.

Relationships are both external and internal to the body. The internal relationships are relationships between the body as a whole and its internal organs and systems. Think of what it means for an organ such as the heart to function properly. It means not only to pump blood but also to pump blood at the appropriate rate moment by moment. Appropriate for what? For the functioning of the body as a whole. So this is a relationship between the heart and the whole body.

External relationships are just as important as internal ones. For example, for the functioning of the body, breathing is essential, and breathing is an active relationship between the body and the air around it.

The person is the complemented body.

But external relationships are important in another way. The **person** is more than the body; it is the body **with its external relationships — the complemented body.** Personal relationships, business relationships, relationships with the nonhuman environment such as the skill of a technician or a tradesman, or a habit of walking in the woods — **all these are features of what the person is.**

For a human being, functioning is functioning of the complete person, not only the body. The external relationships are more definitive of what the person is than the body or its internal subsystems. The reason for this is that the external relationships, more than anything else, define the person **as a whole.** Thus, those who abuse their body, making it serve external relationships (business for example) are living more functionally as persons than those who make bodily health the primary aim of life. Ideally, the most functional state is a balance that cultivates bodily health as a means towards the functioning of the whole person. The body is to the person somewhat as the heart is to the body. But under practical circumstances and the demands of duty this may not be feasible. And in a case such as the care of children, it is more functional for parents to sacrifice their bodily health if necessary in order to care for their children.

However, although the external relationships primarily **define** the person as a whole, the body primarily

Animal bodies have the greatest total individuality.

identifies the person.

All these relationships, external as well as internal, are relative to the body — **the body is the focus of complementation**. Why is this? The animal body has the greatest concentration of individuality of any class of entities that we know. The individuality of the body itself combines the individualities of its internal organs with the individualities of its functional and structural relationships with those organs and the body's individuality as a whole — the body's **total individuality**. This very great total individuality is what everyone marvels at about the functioning of animal bodies.

The individual person is a complex system; a society is also a complex system; an ecosystem is also a complex system. If any of these systems of individual processes is to survive for very long, its components must be mutually functional over the system as a whole — they must not only maintain their own individualities but also be so organized in their external relationships that they contribute to the individualities of the others. Otherwise, their actions in maintaining their own individualities will be at the expense of factors in the individualities of others. In other words, mutual non-functionality as a tendency amounts to mutual counter-functionality in its effects.

This statement may seem implausible with reference to an ecosystem, where predation against other species and defence of territories against other members of one's own are common. But these seemingly counter-functional relationships are combined with other factors to make an overall mutual functionality. Prey species are mostly very prolific in reproduction, and without predators would exhaust their food supply. Territorial defence has the same effect of preventing the overuse of resources, which would result in either a general condition of ill health or a collapse of the population.

But nature is very imperfect in terms of mutual functionality. In general, what is necessary for viability does not necessarily occur. Catastrophes are common in wild life. Epidemics periodically decimate particular species, predators over-hunt their prey and consequently suffer starvation themselves, following which the prey recover, and so on. Nature is not geared to making life pleasant or prosperous for its participants but to realizing the immediate potentiality with greatest individuality. But the same tendency leads to recovery from catastrophes, either for a species or for the ecosystem.

The tendency to make life pleasant and prosperous for its participants is a peculiarity of moral communities, which are peculiar to the social animals.

Opportunistic Individuality:

Individuality is not a global tendency to maximize individuality but a locally opportunistic one, that is, the immediate potentiality with the highest individuality tends to be the one that is realized (in accordance with the principle of causality by patterns). The tendency is to climb the steepest immediate gradient of potentialities for individuality. This is not a tendency for things to "work out for the best" but for immediate opportunities for individuality to be taken, regardless of their larger-scale or longer-term effects. As we all know, if a person is to pursue their long-term benefit, they must have learned to have that benefit immediately in view, so that the attraction of the long-term benefit outweighs the attraction of incompatible short-term pleasures. In other words, the long-term potentialities have to be turned into immediate tendencies by conceptual means.

This basic tendency can take pathological forms. For example, if one has developed a self-concept as a failure, or as one whom the world is against, an opportunity that would normally hold out a prospect for a gain of individuality may be rejected in bitterness. How does this follow the maximum gradient of individuality? The answer is that confirming one's self-concept

Immediate gains of individuality

provides a greater immediate gain (or a smaller loss) of individuality than taking an opportunity at which one expects to fail.

The emergence of new individualities is governed by the same opportunism. When an animal body is weakened through stress or malnutrition, microorganisms find niches

New individualities occupy niches,

where they can thrive at the expense of the animal. When an animal dies, carrion feeders and microorganisms quickly feed on the defenceless carcass. In a large organization, if serving the interests of the organization does not fully realize the individuality of individuals, they begin to find other ways of doing so, such

if there is sustenance.

as building their own small empires within the organization. In society at large, if the opportunity to live as parasites rather than as contributors to the common welfare presents itself, many will take that opportunity (from a cost-benefit point of view, disregarding ethical considerations, it is more efficient). And most will take the opportunity to live as partial parasites.

The issue of sustenance is important here. What gives living organisms their very high levels of total individuality is their functional complexity, including a rich set of functional external relationships. A function is a process passing from one process to another (or to itself). Therefore, these external relationships involve the passage of materials and energy into and out of the body or the person. That being so, an external supply of the needed materials is necessary to maintain the individuality of the body and the person. I put it in these terms to point to the fact that sustenance is not only food in the ordinary sense, but whatever needs to be imported into the body or the complemented body in order to maintain the individuality of the body and the person, as, for example, new furniture for one's house. For the person, what that sustenance is depends on the particular acquired needs of the person's individuality.

In human life, whenever sustenance for the body and the person is available and existing circumstances leave an apparent deficit of individuality of the body or the person, the person will tend to avail itself of that sustenance to develop a new and more effective means of maximizing its individuality. This tendency varies widely because of the complexity and wide variety of human individualities.

That variety also takes the form of the changing individuality of an individual person moment by moment. This is the individuality of the person's relationships and is governed by the need for individuality in relation to other persons and also to inanimate things, for example in the exercise of a skill. Its opportunistic character consists in the fact that it is a response to changes in other persons or things.

What holds for individuals holds also for communities, but for a somewhat different reason. Communities do not have the high levels of total individuality that individual animals have. But the shared interests of individuals are vested in communities and their institutions, so that through the actions of the members and the dynamics of their individualities, communities in effect act so as to maximize their individualities, that is, to maximize the individualities of their members (perhaps of certain privileged members).

The same for communities

Thus, when a nation appears (to its leaders) to be threatened as to its vital interests, it seeks ways of counteracting the threat, by war if other means appear ineffective. General peace will be achieved when no nation or tribe feels threatened as to its vital interests.

Another example: just as rich individuals exploit poor individuals, so rich nations exploit poor nations, so that the citizens of the rich nations may have the pleasures of affluence. In both cases, self-justification motivates a pretence of serving the interests of the poor. In the world of the year 2001, if you look just a little below the surface, you see that the old-style colonialism has not been virtuously abandoned but transformed into a multinational economic colonialism. Here the rich nations are analogous to germs and the poor nations to the weakened body.

The only thing that alters this pattern is ethics. It does so by adding another class of objects of opportunistic individuality to the primary object, so that the basic tendency of following the maximal gradient of one's own potential individuality includes a tendency to maximize the individualities of other members of one's moral community.

Health:

Health in the fullest sense is the health of the complete person. If we had to define health in one sentence, the accepted definition would probably be that it is the ability to function. To be ill or impaired is to be unable to function fully. On this basis the health of the body would be its ability to function in relation to the person, the health of the heart would be its ability to function in relation to the body, and the health of the person would be its ability to function in relation to itself and external entities.

> **Health is functioning**

For the heart to function in relation to the body is to contribute actively to the individuality of the body — to its **being**, and as Aristotle says, the "being" of something includes its functioning. For the body to function in relation to the person is to contribute to the person's being or individuality. For the person to function in relation to itself is to contribute to its own individuality — to be functional rather than dysfunctional. To be dysfunctional is to contribute to its own disintegration.

> **To function is to contribute to individuality.**

But health is more than that. To be healthy is to be well — **well-being**. Thus, health is not only functioning but also the benefit of functioning — actual individuality.

This tells us something about the various dimensions of health. They are the levels of functionality and the levels of well-being or individuality.

FUNCTIONALITY
of subsystems of the body relative to the body
of the body relative to the person
of external relationships relative to the body
of external relationships relative to the person
INDIVIDUALITY

of the body
of the person

These facets of health are all in the category of the **ability** to live well. But health is not only the ability to live well but also **actually** living well — wholeness and distinctiveness of living. **Vitality** is a suitable word for the quantity or degree of **ability** to live well, while **vivacity** is a suitable word for the quantity or degree of actually living well, the degree of individuality of **actually living**. Actually living is of the present moment, the living present. It is in the category of the creative factor's action, the category of change. Consequently it does not have individuality in the way that a structure or a process in temporal space does. Its individuality consists of variations of individuality — gains and losses of individuality — gains and losses of wholeness or distinctiveness. As a quantity, vivacity is the sum of the gains minus the losses of individuality in the present moment. These gains and losses of individuality will be gains and losses in one or more of the dimensions of vitality. Positive vivacity is a gain of vitality.

Vivacity = gains of vitality - losses of vitality

Gains of vitality are of two kinds: The course of events in the life of a person is divided into phases which have individuality, and there are individual phases within individual phases. For example, a day is a phase with a degree of individuality; within that phase there are changes of activity separating individual phases of activity, such as working at a particular task, taking a coffee break, working at another task, and so on. Within each of these phases are shorter phases as one turns one's attention to different things. Within one such phase the activity may be such as to increase or decrease vitality in one respect or another. For example, working when fatigued may reduce one's vitality.

But the **occurrence** of a new phase of activity is itself a gain of individuality, since that phase itself has individuality. Its cessation, however, is not a loss of individuality, since its individuality continues to exist and becomes part of the person's total individuality as that phase recedes into the past. It is lost from the living present, but not from vitality.

A consequence of this is that the exercise of vitality itself increases that vitality, provided it falls within certain bounds beyond which it would be harmful. The implication is that actually living is not only an aspect of health but is healthy in its effects. **Vivacity is not only healthy in itself but also healthy for the person.**

These facets of health are not all of the same importance. Functionality serves individuality and is for the sake of individuality or well-being. But well-being has the two aspects of vitality and vivacity. Vitality is the capability of living. Therefore, vitality is for the sake of living, and the intensity or richness of living is vivacity.

Moreover, if functionality is for the sake of the individuality it furthers, then the vivacity of the body's subsystems is for the sake of the vivacity of the body, and the body's vivacity and the vivacity of its external relationships are for the sake of the vivacity of the person.

So we may fill out the chart of the dimensions of health as follows:

The Dimensions of Health

Vitality
(Capacity for living)
Functionality:
Of subsystems of the body relative to the body
Of the body relative to the person
Of the external relationships relative to the body
Of external relationships relative to the body
Of external relationships relative to the person
Integrity
(Individuality as a whole body and/or whole person)
For the sake of
Vivacity
(Actual living)
Vivacity of subsystems of the body
For the sake of
Vivacity of the body & vivacity of external relationships
For the sake of
Vivacity of the person

The Present Moment:

Vivacity measures changes in vitality in the present moment. What is that present moment? You have to think in terms of processes in temporal space. This means thinking graphically; think of a picture or diagram of past, present, and future. Ideally, this is a four-dimensional picture, but most of us are not able to visualize four dimensions. However, we can compress the three spatial dimensions into one, so that the picture of temporal space is only two-dimensional. This can still convey a useful, though inadequate, impression of processes in temporal space.

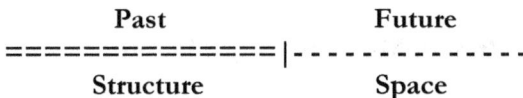

Past	**Future**
=============| - - - - - - - - - - - - -	
Structure	**Space**

If you think of a structure growing into the empty space in front of it, the future is the empty space in front of it, and the process up to that point is already in the past. So on this basis (leaving out tendencies), the present moment is only the instant of the coming into existence of another particle. This is thinking in terms of structure and change only.

However, when you bring tendency into the picture, the present moment suddenly acquires size and substance. The present moment is the time when tendencies are active — when forces are alive — in the past they are dead.

Active tendencies define the present moment.

Tendencies are the tendencies of processes in temporal space, processes with histories and potential futures. For example, you have a tendency to stop working and go for lunch; this is a tendency of someone who has worked through the morning and looks forward to a leisurely lunch. In other words, the scope of the tendency extends back through the morning and forward through the lunch hour.

Tendencies are both short-term and long-term; for example we make plans covering our lifetime or beyond. And at the other extreme, the tendencies of microscopic processes extend only minute fractions of a second into the past and future.

This shows that the present moment is not just one single thing. Rather,

Present extends into past and future.

there is a present moment for each process or sub-process that has an active tendency, one for the person, one for the body, one for each relationship of the body, one for each molecule-process, one for each atom-process, one for each particle-process.

The present moment of a complex process such as a person is made up of the many present moments of the many sub-processes within it. Its overall extent is that of the longest-term tendency.

```
=========={={=={={=|-}--}--}---}------
```

Past   {   **Present Moment**   }   **Future**

Change is ongoing, and as minimal events go by, the sub-processes or phases of sub-processes with active tendencies are altered, new ones begin, and others are terminated. These changes bring gains and losses of individuality. These phase changes, with a variety of frequencies, amount to a complicated variation of individuality, somewhat resembling "white noise" but organized rather than random. The effect of this is normally a net gain of individuality, and the higher the average frequency of the variations the greater the net gain.

Argument for this: The termination of a process does not reduce its individuality. Just as death does not eliminate the individuality of a person, so the termination of a distinctive phase of a sub-process does not eliminate its individuality nor constitute a loss of individuality for the larger process.

Termination of a sub-process is not a loss of individuality.

However, the occurrence of a new sub-process is a gain of individuality, by the amount of the individuality of the new sub-process.

But the occurrence of a new sub-process is a gain.

Consequently, the more frequent the changes of phase are, the greater is the vivacity (provided the phases themselves are not losses of individuality). This is related to the significance of excitation, excitement, and subtlety for the understanding of vivacity, health, and stress.

Excitation:

Excitation is a continuing stimulus that generates changes in the activity of a process (the person being the process of interest), such as a situation in which interesting things are happening. The effect of such a stimulus is a variety of distinctive phases in the activity of the person, hence a high state of vivacity. This is an effect on the various sub-processes of the body and its external relationships. Consequently, it

Sensational entertainments make less vivacity than subtle ones.

involves a variety of overlapping phase sequences of various frequencies.

We have seen just now that the higher the frequency of such an effect the higher the vivacity. What this means in practical terms is that the subtler forms of excitation result in higher vivacity than the cruder forms.

Excitement:

Excitement is excitation of a comparatively crude sort, characterized by powerful stimuli on a fairly large scale (in comparison with the range of time-scales of the human body). Sensational entertainments are exciting, but they are not productive of high vivacity, comparatively.

But of course there are exceptions to that statement. The key word here is **variety**. Variety in the environment calls for changes in the character of the person's responses. This starts a complex train of internal processes, with phase changes on a variety of time scales. The result is the maximization of the frequency of changes of phase and the maximization of the increases minus the decreases of individuality.

The implication for health is that a variety of situations (work, play, entertainments of a variety of sorts, emphasizing the subtler ones) is healthiest. And this is because the level of vivacity of the person is the final criterion of health. The functionality of the system **is** functionality because of its contribution to the vivacity of the person.

There is an important difference between externally driven excitation and internally driven excitation (relative to the body). Either of these may be due to factors that are either functional or counter-functional relative to the body or the person. Externally driven excitation imposes the individuality of external relationships and of the person on the body. Internally driven excitation is excitation driven by the body's own tendency to maximize its individuality; this is recuperation from the stress of work or play. When that recuperation is accomplished, that same tendency leads the system to seek external excitation.

What is stress?

In the scientific sense of the word, stress is an action applied to a system that the system must respond to so as to avoid suffering a loss of individuality. Taking the word in that sense, stress may be either beneficial or harmful. But taking the word in its popular sense of a harmful stimulus or activity, stress is an excess of some one kind of excitation — that is,

Variety is important for health.

Vitality is capacity for vivacity.

beyond the point of positive vivacity into negative vivacity, a net loss of individuality. It is most commonly understood as an excess of some form of externally driven excitation — work or personal troubles. But excessive relaxation can also be stressful, the symptom being boredom and restlessness. This harms the person and even the body.

Again, the key word is **variety**; we need a variety of situations and activities in order to optimize health. But variety can also be excessive; it must be variety within the scope of a repetitiveness that defines what the person is, individuality in the qualitative sense.

An important point here is this: the higher the level of individuality, the wider the variations of which it is capable (since there is more of it that can vary). Consequently, the greater one's vitality is, the greater vivacity one is capable of. The higher one's level of functionality and individuality are, the greater is one's capacity for excitement as well as for the subtler forms of excitation. The person who is constantly seeking sensational excitements thereby develops a

And enjoyment of enhanced living.

lower level of vitality of external relationships than the person who seeks a wider variety of excitations, emphasizing the subtler ones. Consequently, the sensation seeker has less capacity for excitement than the person who usually seeks subtler pleasures.

External Relationships:

External relationships more than other aspects of the person define what the person as a whole is (you are your personal relationships, your work, your position in society, your responsibilities). And the other aspects of health are for the sake of the vivacity of the person — for the sake of the intensity of actual living.

When people think of **living** in an emphatic sense, they usually (it seems) think of it as self-indulgence and seeking excitements and powerful sensations.

This is not a very perceptive notion of living intensely. Living intensely (as a person) is maximizing

Not excitement but external functionality.

the vivacity of one's external relationships. Those relationships are relationships in both directions. How you act in relation to other persons, institutions, or the non-human environment, affects how any of these act in relation to you. So the vivacity of the relationship is not only a property of your actions but of the response of the other relata as well. If you are a parent, neglecting your children to pursue other "pleasures" is not the way to maximize the vivacity of your relationships. Maximizing the vivacity of your relationships is maximizing their **functionality**, their tendency to increase the individuality of the other relata, which will then tend to increase your own individuality as a person (and vivacity is gains of individuality). In the case of personal relationships, facilitating the individualities of the other persons also increases your own. Think of a number of individual processes interacting in complex ways. If they relate to one another in predominantly functional ways, the result is a general maximization of individuality. But if they relate to one another in predominantly counter-functional ways, the result is a general minimization of individuality. And in the latter case, each of them, faced with enemies all round, will defend itself by relating to the others even more counter-functionally. Each of these is a self-reinforcing condition, with no stable intermediate condition. The tendency of functionality is to move to greater functionality; the tendency of counter-functionality is to move to greater counter-functionality.

Why, then, would anyone ever act counter-functionally relative to others? The primary tendency is to maximize one's own individuality, and this is first of all serving the needs of one's body. This may be in competition with the same tendency in others. Consequently, for the mutually functional behaviour to prevail the individuals need to perceive that the mutually functional behaviour will better serve the needs of their bodies than a selfish mode of behaviour that ignores the question of its effects on others.

Mind & Body:

The common distinction between mental health and bodily health is pretty clear: mental health is the capacity for functioning in the outside world, as well as actually functioning in it — bodily health pertains to the internal relationships of the body, and mental health pertains to its external relationships. On this basis, the distinction between body and mind is the distinction between the body's internal relationships and its external relationships.

Nowadays the common conception is that the mind is in the brain. This is about a half-truth at most. If you think about the actual content of a developed mind and where that content is stored, books, computer disks, and other repositories of information come to mind. Information in these repositories may be more accessible than much of what is stored in the brain. But apart from such intellectual information, a vast amount of information is contained in the common environment in the form of vegetation, stones, streets, buildings, animals, and other not easily classified things. A good deal of that information is mirrored in our brains in an abbreviated form, but by far the bulk of it is accessed by us through ongoing perception.

What then? If the mind is where its information is, we have to say that it is both internal and external to our bodies, and the more developed the mind is the more of it is external.

But if we understand the mind to be active in managing the information of interest to the person, then we have to locate the mind in the relationship between the body (with emphasis on the brain) and its environment. Certainly, a lot of that activity takes place in the brain, but

The mind is in the body's external relationships.

equally important are the sensory functions and the body's motor functions in orienting itself to objects and manipulating them. So the mind is an aspect of the body's external relationships.

I am refraining from offering a definition of "mind", because I think the concept is more useful in its vague and ambiguous popular form.

Psychosomatic Effects:

The popular meaning of "psychosomatic" is "the effects of the mind on the body". This has two varieties, the effects of external relationships on internal relationships, & the effects of a special external relationship, namely complementation with the creative factor (God and the will) on internal relationships.

These belong to a larger class, namely the effects on bodily subsystems of **their** external relationships. Their external relationships include the external relationships of larger subsystems and of the body. In other words, "psychosomatic" can be taken to refer to effects of larger subsystems or of the whole person on smaller subsystems.

Concrete relationships are not merely **between** their relata in an exclusive sense. They penetrate their relata according to the nature of the relationship. For example, breathing is a relationship between the body and its surrounding atmosphere, reaching into the air outside and the lungs inside. Seeing reaches to an external object and involves the whole body as one orients oneself to the object and reacts to what one sees. In this way external relationships have direct effects on the internal workings of the body.

But the term "psychosomatic" applies more appropriately where the external relationships of a subsystem are a factor in defining its individuality and determining its level of individuality. For example, the function of the pancreas in regulating blood sugar levels is an external relationship of the pancreas; dietary habits that cause instabilities of blood sugar level, which in turn cause diabetes would then be psychosomatic factors damaging the pancreas. These are relationships of complementation. Health is individuality and gains of individuality, and relationships that contribute to determining the degree of a subsystem's individuality are factors in its health, and factors in its health are factors in the whole person's health.

When psychosomatic effects are understood in this way, as effects of the external relationships of subsystems on those subsystems, their subtlety and elusiveness becomes understandable. And we then see where to look in investigating them.

Modes of Complementation:

We can get some insight into these relationships by looking into the nature of complementation — relationships that define individuality as a whole. There are several modes of complementation — structural, kinetic, dynamic, by similarity to patterns, by similarity as a pattern to potentialities, and animate (relations with the creative factor).

These relationships have their own degrees of wholeness and distinctiveness, and since they are relationships of the body, those degrees of individuality are imposed on the complemented body.

Structural: The external relationships that define the person have spatial properties that are then imposed on the body as its spatial or structural relationships. For example, being involved in global business imposes structural relations on the body relating it to distant places around the globe. This has the effect of "stretching" the body, of forcing it into perceptual relations foreign to its normal capabilities. This is probably a form of stress detrimental to bodily health. We must remember, however, that health is not primarily bodily health but the health of the person.

Kinetic: (Structural Relations in Motion): Watch a cat moving about. Its bodily motions, both in themselves and in relation to its surroundings, illustrate wholeness and distinctiveness of kinetic relationships. A walk in the woods for most people heals the ill effects of workaday stress. This is partly because of the wholeness and distinctiveness of the structural and kinetic relationships that such a walk produces.

Dynamic: (Shared or Relational Tendencies): When two people work together on a mechanical task, they draw the tendencies that govern their ongoing actions from the task itself and the way it brings them into relationship. In that situation what they are individually is partially defined and completed by the shared tendencies of that dynamic relationship. This is dynamic complementation. Emotions such as love, hate, envy, jealousy, pity, are in part tendencies due to relations between persons and affecting those relations and each of the persons. Clearly, relations of dynamic complementation are factors in the health of the person and affect the health of the body. Again, this is because the external relationships of the body penetrate the body and are relationships of the entire body. External tendencies relating the person to other persons, for example, impose their tendency towards a gain or a loss of individuality on the body as well as on the person. Thus, love, goodwill, hope, exhilaration, are conducive to bodily health, while resentment, malice, despair, and depression are destructive of it.

Similarity to Patterns: Structural, kinetic, and dynamic complementation are familiar and obvious to normal perception. Complementation by similarity with patterns is not apparent to normal perception except in those cases where the patterns are objects of conscious experience, such as an influential personal example. But according to causality by patterns and the principle of complementation, an important component of what one is is one's rootedness in the many patterns presented by the universe and its history. And the one facet of this rootedness that does arouse some people's interest is complementation by similarity with individual persons in the past (either real or imagined). But equally important is complementation by similarity with the necessary patterns. This determines one's fundamental nature, not as a human being but as a process in temporal space, as sharing the basic and permanent nature of all material things.

These relations of similarity with patterns are transcendent — they are mediated by the creative factor, which makes the comparisons. Notice that similarity is not a concrete relation between things in temporal space itself without the creative factor. Two things are simply two things with their respective properties; their similarity becomes a concrete relation only when some agent compares them — "sees" properties of one in the other. Similarity is not a structural relation, but it is like a structural relation in that it connects two things at different places in temporal space. But it does so by a route that leaves temporal space and returns to it, via the creative factor. We may call similarity a para-structural relation.

The rootedness of a person also answers to the concept of soul. One's soul is one's nature in the deepest sense, in other words one's most enduring and embracing tendencies. This is ambiguous. It can be the soul of the entire person, that is, all the tendencies of all kinds of the body or complemented body; this includes rootedness in necessary patterns. It can be the soul of the body as a whole, which is mainly rootedness in biological patterns. Or it can be the soul of the person as a whole, and this is the more common notion of soul. The person as a whole is primarily the body's external relationships, so that the soul of the person as a whole is primarily the rootedness of the body's external relationships (personal, business, etc.). The patterns for that rootedness include some necessary patterns, especially those supporting individuality, but the interesting ones from a popular point of view, are similar relationships in lives in the past. A sense of this form of rootedness has given rise to the notion of reincarnation, a notion that is plausible in cases where the person as a whole is very similar to some person as a whole in the past. But this concept of soul has more commonplace applications. One's major external relationships include occupations and professions and the positions one takes on in these functions, as well as parenthood or other functional relationships of a voluntary nature — in short, one's responsibilities. Adolescents and young adults are occupied in selecting what their responsibilities will be. But most of these responsibilities have been prepared for them in the form of examples of such responsibilities, present and past, and opportunities for assuming them (potentialities matching those patterns). In other words, the community prepares potential souls for its young people, and their similarities as potentialities to those patterns constitute their aptitude for having those souls conferred on them.

The person as a whole is the person as a whole in time as well as in space. It comprises the lifetime of the person up to the present moment or up to the time of death. Throughout life the person is shaping its soul, since changing attitudes and actions bring about varying similarities with patterns. Once shaped, that portion of the soul is permanent. One can initiate a trend contrary to the soul one has at a given time, and that reversal is itself an important feature of one's soul. Thus, repentance of an unwholesome past makes its rootedness in patterns a source of aversion.14 However, that past portion of one's soul cannot be eliminated as a factor influencing one's potentialities. Thus, having repented, one is nonetheless apt to relapse. And a similar dynamic applies to a fall from a wholesome portion of soul into an unwholesome portion. Although the wholesome portion has been rejected, it continues to exercise its influence.

Similarity as a Pattern to Potentialities. But a complete person also includes the person's influence through causality by patterns. To be similar to another life in a way that may influence it is a facet of what one is, that is, that relationship of influence is a facet of what one is.

This mode of complementation answers to the concept of one's spirit. The connotation of "spirit" is one's efficacy as a cause through other than material processes. In the present context one's spirit would be one's causal efficacy through causality by patterns, by being a pattern for potentialities.

One is a pattern for potentialities in two ways: as a pattern for other lives and as a pattern for one's own actions and perceptions. The principal pattern for a person's actions and perceptions is that same person. One's actions and perceptions are characteristic of oneself — "in the spirit" of the person. To be "spirited" is to set a powerful example for one's own continued living. To be "in high spirits" is to feel one's capability for action intensely.

To be aware of one's spirit is to be aware of oneself as immediately sensitive and active and as a ubiquitous presence, now and throughout all future time, potentially influencing the lives that may exist at any given time and place.

14See "Emotion & Feeling" in "Consciousness, Choice, & Reasoning".

Animate: The transcendent relationships Creation, Truth, Beneficence, Rootedness, and Influence are essential to our existence and nature. These are relationships of complementation with the creative factor, or in the cases of Rootedness and Influence (soul and spirit), through the creative factor. St. Paul's statement that "in God we live and move and have our being" is pretty accurate. One feels Creation as a sense of being actuated by something transcendent and of acting by one's own volition (the first of these in unconscious life and the second in consciousness). One feels Truth as one's conscience enjoining one to be truthful. One feels Beneficence as one's instinct for maximizing one's individuality and also as one's desire for the individualities of others. One feels Rootedness as one's soul. And one feels Influence as the power of action and thought and also as responsibility for future generations.

Person-to-Person Interactions: This is complementation between two or more personal animate complementations. The consciousness of another person as a person is a consciousness of that person's complementation with the creative factor, as having will, conscience, goodwill (or ill will), soul, and spirit. As such it is also a transcendent relationship, mediated by the creative factor.

Person-to-person relationships are characterized by emotion, emotions of harmony or dissonance, love or hate, approval or disapproval. These presuppose that the other person is a volitional agent with an individuality comprising all the aspects just mentioned as complementations of an animate body. It is that individuality that elicits emotions peculiar to person-to-person relationships — emotions of desire to share some of those transcendent relationships, perhaps to increase one's own individuality by assimilating that of the other, emotions of respect or reverence, or scorn, or fear of being engulfed. Person-to-person relationships are very different from person-to-thing relationships. A mere "thing" has tendencies but none of the other transcendent relationships just mentioned, whereas person-to-person relationships are emotion-to-emotion, will-to-will, conscience-to-conscience, spirit-to-spirit, and soul-to-soul.

Amoral persons are unable to experience this contrast. The "warmth" of friendly encounters, and similarly the "chill" of hostile encounters or being in the presence of malice or amorality, is due to consciousness of the will and moral attitude of the other. Amoral persons are insensitive to these factors.[15]

These modes of complementation are important for many reasons, but I introduced them under the heading of psychosomatic effects. The person is the complemented body. The person's relationships are also the body's relationships. The individuality of these relationships is imposed on the individuality of the person, since the person as a whole is defined primarily by

---

[15]See "The Fourth Form of Moral Degeneracy (the Amoral Person)" in "Ethics & Self-Validation".

external relationships. Accordingly, they are imposed on the complemented body and the internal systems of the body. This is pretty obvious in the case of structural, kinetic, and dynamic complementation. A well-proportioned distribution of furniture in a room large enough not to seem cramped and small enough to seem protective makes for comfort and easy movement. This is in harmony with the functioning of the body, which is largely why it makes for comfort and easy movement. For the same reason it is conducive to bodily health. And a room with properties in contrast with these is neither comfortable nor healthy. A neighbourhood environment in which one can habitually move about in ways that have wholeness and distinctiveness and that help to define one's individuality as a person is conducive to both personal health and bodily health. This will be a neighbourhood in which there are places that invite the casual congregation of neighbours. And that casual congregation is an example of dynamic complementation that has individuality — emotional relationships with qualities of wholeness and distinctiveness.

The same is true for complementation by similarity as a pattern to other lives. To know that one's example is having a wholesome effect on someone else is the best encouragement to maintaining and improving that example, and a part of that is living in a manner that will be wholesome for one's body.

And of course being influenced by good examples can only be conducive to individuality at all levels. The reason is that individuality is the same wherever it occurs, although its particulars may be very different; consequently examples of it are effective patterns for it even though the pattern may be very different from the potentiality in other respects.

An interesting case of a psychosomatic effect due to similarity to a pattern is the use of "imaging" to combat a disease or promote bodily health in some way. Here the image one thinks of is a pattern for a process of healing. How effective it is depends on the person's skill in setting up a similarity between the pattern and the potentiality for healing. But the subtlety of psychosomatic effects is such that knowing that may not be of much help toward developing such a skill.

Another example is what I will call **the good behaviour reflex**. When one is in company and desirous of being presentable, bodily systems that might cause one embarrassment work better than in more relaxed circumstances. This is observable in hospital patients when their neighbours come to visit. The same, of course, is true, perhaps less uniformly, of components of personality and moral character. Most people, in a situation where they wish to make a good impression, put on a better character than they really have.

Does God Have Individuality?

God according to the present account is the creative factor as related to the world by the transcendent relationships Creation, Truth, Rootedness, Influence, and Beneficence (within Rootedness).

- ❑ The creative factor itself is not a process, not being in temporal space, but the complemented creative factor (as related to the world through these transcendent relationships) is many processes, one for each distinctive process, since the concrete content of these relationships is always changing.
- ❑ Beneficence is a functional relationship, the fundamental source of individuality in individual processes.
- ❑ Beneficence as a relationship of the creative factor with a particular individual process has a greater degree of individuality than it causes in the target process, for the following reasons:
  - o The part of the relationship that is internal to the target process has the degree of individuality that Beneficence causes.
  - o The other relata of the relationship (the necessary patterns Particle and Discreteness) are the paradigms of individuality, the patterns of individuation of which individuality is only an analogue. Instead of wholeness and distinctiveness, they have perfect singleness and separateness.
- ❑ Then, since Beneficence is a relationship that partially defines what God is, its individuality confers individuality on God.

The conclusion that God has individuality in relation to us prepares the ground for later showing that God is a member of every moral community.

The Imperfection of Individuality:

Individuality is subject to degrees. Perfect individuality would be 100% similarity with Particle and Discreteness. Only a particle can have this. But there can be a simulation of perfect individuality based on an arbitrary criterion that one may satisfy to perfection or virtual perfection.

We see exemplified at least two forms of such a criterion:

1. Taking oneself as the criterion. In that case one certainly meets the criterion, and no one else does.
2. Taking general competence in living as the criterion.

These are means of achieving self-validation, but the price is taking a counterfeit of individuality as one's criterion of personal success.

1. In the first case the counterfeit is patent, and the price is an extreme state of self-deception, which is in need of constant repair as the truth keeps coming into one's consciousness. We take amusement from such persons, but they are to be pitied.

2. The second case is more insidious. Offhand, general competence in living is obviously desirable — knowing how to set priorities in accordance with real value, and being able to attain them without committing blunders. The paradigm of this criterion is the person who "can't afford to make mistakes". It is true: we cannot afford to make mistakes with regard to the most important things in life. But honesty might tell us that losing what we cannot afford to lose and suffering what we cannot afford to suffer are the common and unavoidable vicissitudes of life.

The proof that something is wrong is that general competence in living is not the same as individuality. And individuality is nature's criterion of success — genuine success as an individual process.

But perhaps general competence in living is a practical aim that may result in as high a level of individuality as one is capable of. Is this true?

High competence in life and setting a high value on high competence in life would lead us to approach life as a technical skill (concentrating on "getting it right"). Such competence is impossible, since individuality is not something one can "get right". But something like it may be possible, something that one would mistake for it, namely, a construal of success in life as something other than individuality, something one can "get right", with the cultivation of the skill of "getting it right" by that criterion. This state of mind is not so uncommon.

What is wrong with this attitude? Apart from being a false notion of the success of an individual process, it deprives one of the deepest enjoyments of life. To take life seriously implies valuing and cultivating its deep emotions (emotions of appreciation of the sacredness of individualities). The common major griefs of life are a principal stimulus arousing these emotions and reminding us of the sacredness of individualities. But if one's criterion of success in living is something other than individuality, one will not see those emotions and that reminder as a benefit; one is more likely to take pride in rising above life's griefs. Hence one will not value these deep emotions and will not be sensitive to them. And one will value one's own competence more than the individualities of others.

The irony of individuality is that accepting its imperfection is essential to achieving the greatest enjoyments of life. This is not to say that the common griefs of life are to be accounted as goods, rather that the emotions associated with recognizing the sacredness of individuality (which these griefs can give us) are among the chief goods of life. They are instances of high conscious vivacity — large conscious gains of individuality.

11 CONSCIOUSNESS, CHOICE, & REASONING

Consciousness is an important feature of our nature, and has even been thought by some to constitute all of it. But a little observation makes it clear that much of our life is not within the scope of our consciousness. For example, we are unconscious of most of what goes on inside our bodies.

How is it that some of what we do and experience we do and experience consciously and the rest not? What makes the difference, and how is consciousness possible at all?

First, what is it we are asking about? What are we referring to when we ask about consciousness? We must answer this in phenomenological terms, that is, in terms of consciousness itself, not in terms of the material conditions of consciousness.

❑ We are not unaware of the aspects of our life of which we are unconscious, but this is an indirect awareness mediated by observation and inferences. For example, we know about our brain through science.

❑ Consciousness, by contrast is immediate, transparent, and concentrated separately on some object or situation.

❑ What does "transparent" mean? In consciousness we "see through" our consciousness of an object to the object and "see into" the object. For example, we see into the space around us, not as if it were one thing and our consciousness were another, but through our consciousness as the medium reaching from our point of view to the object. By contrast, when we are told of an event, we

Consciousness is immediate, transparent, & focussed.

53

reconstruct that event in imagination, that is, we construct a representation of it. Then we "see through" our consciousness of that representation and "see into" the representation.

Objection: It is usually thought that consciousness is a representation of its real objects and not immediate at all.

❑ Consciousness may represent things one is not immediately conscious of. In that case the representation is the immediate object of consciousness. But when we are conscious of an object present to our perception, the immediate object of consciousness is the real object (the tree, for example) **as responded to by the person** (as looked at, as handled, as approached, as avoided, as thought about). That object (the tree *as responded to by the person*) is experienced immediately and transparently. **It is the response that is immediate, transparent, and concentrated separately on the object.**

❑ Thus, consciousness of a concrete object such as a tree is a relationship between the person and the tree, so that the location of consciousness of an external object is in the space between one's body and the object, inclusive. Consciousness is not located in the brain, although the brain is an essential factor in the relationship that constitutes consciousness. Consciousness is where its object and its point of view are.

❑ By contrast, our awareness of the aspects of our life of which we are not conscious (say the workings of our nerves) has no such form. Instead, we **represent** it in consciousness as a product of observation and reasoning — for the most part as a product of science acquired second-hand. And the representation is then the immediate object of consciousness.

❑ But even consciousness of an object that is not present is a relationship with one's environment. Experiments with sensory deprivation have shown how consciousness becomes distorted and dysfunctional when that relationship is suspended.

❑ A person's concentrated response to an object is just as real a part of the universe as the object itself as a separate thing. And the tree as an object of consciousness is the same real tree that was

Consciousness is not mere appearance

there before the person looked at it, only in relation to the person rather than as a separate thing. Indeed, particular things apart from their relations with other things are abstractions from reality, which consists of things in relation to one another. Consciousness is not mere appearance as distinguished from reality but a special kind of relationship between a person and an object.

Why are we conscious, and what makes it possible?

In terms of evolution and natural selection, living organisms need to be able to make concentrated responses to particular local events, either because they are dangerous or because they present opportunities to obtain food. This is the **functionality** of the conditions for consciousness. But the fact that consciousness would be advantageous does not imply that it exists. We know it exists, but theoretically life might not have been possible at all. What is it in the constitution of the universe that makes consciousness and life possible?

The creative factor is conscious of the universe. That is, it responds to the universe immediately and transparently, just as it is.[16] This is different from **our** consciousness in that it is not focussed on any particular object or situation, nor does it have any point of view. But if **we** were to respond to the entire universe immediately and transparently, we would say we were conscious of it. Therefore, we should also say that the creative factor is conscious of the universe.

The creative factor's consciousness of the universe is what makes our consciousness possible. Without it materialism would be the case, and there is no place in materialism for consciousness.

The creative factor is conscious of the universe.

How does the creative factor's consciousness become an individual person's consciousness?

The creative factor's consciousness of the universe has to be localized and identified with the individual person. The following conditions bring this about:

1. The person responds to an object or situation in a way that is concentrated **exclusively** on it, leaving other objects out. (For example, one looks at a book and focuses on a particular paragraph.) This is the same as saying that one's response has individuality.

---

[16]See "Causality by Patterns".

2. The object is the circumstance of a gain or loss of the person's individuality. This brings the object within the scope of the person's individuality, so that the response has the property of **immediacy**.

All events are actions of the creative factor, and the creative factor effectuates the person's response exactly as it is, **exclusively** and **immediately** according to the two conditions just stated.

☐ The creative factor's effectuation is also a component of the creative factor's consciousness.

The creative factor's consciousness becomes the person's consciousness.

☐ As the effectuation of the person's response it is the person's response.

☐ Under the above conditions (1. & 2.) the response is exclusive and immediate.

☐ Therefore, it is the person's consciousness.

Consciousness has Degrees:

What makes consciousness vivid or intense? Each of the two conditions for consciousness listed above (1. & 2.) has degrees.

☐ The person's response to an object or situation may be more or less exclusive of other objects — more or less concentrated. This affects the vividness of consciousness, the degree to which the object is sharply defined.

Focus affects vividness.

❏ The concentration of the response is affected by the nature of the object. A sharply defined object such as a poster with a printed message on it will elicit a more vivid consciousness than a less well-defined one such as variations of dust on a wall (other things being equal).

Gain or loss of individuality affects intensity.

☐ The gain or loss of

individuality may be greater or smaller. In other words, the object or situation may interest the person to a greater or less degree. This affects the intensity of consciousness.

- ❏ For example, one is more intensely conscious of a situation that promises great pleasure or distress than of one that offers no particular prospect of further gains or losses of individuality. This second condition expresses the functionality of consciousness. One is intensely conscious of circumstances that seriously affect one's vital interests and that demand a response.

- ☐ However, if the gain or loss of individuality is too great, especially in the case of a loss, consciousness is temporarily impossible. This is a state of shock.
  - ❏ The reason for this is that a change of circumstances that would bring an extreme gain or loss of individuality is not immediately integrated with the current state of the person as an individual process, so that the process istemporarily terminated with respect to its external relationships. Consequently, there is no object to be responded to exclusively.
  - ❏ The intensity of consciousness will also affect its vividness. To see this, consider that an object of virtually no interest has correspondingly little effect on one's consciousness, and a very low level of consciousness cannot be very intense. Nor can it be very vivid.
  - ❏ **This tells us that the gain or loss of individuality (the degree to which one's interest is engaged) is the fundamental cause of consciousness and determines its level of intensity, while the distinctiveness of its object elicits its degree of vividness within the range permitted by its intensity.**

Emotion & Feeling:

Emotions are experiences of how one's interests are affected by circumstances. Thus, the causes of emotion are comparisons of individuality and of potentialities for individuality. These include comparisons over time, in other words gains or losses of individuality or of

Emotion, the primary mode of consciousness

potentialities for individuality, and comparisons of one's own potentialities with those of others. Elation and alarm are experiences of gains and losses of individuality respectively. Envy and disdainfulness are experiences of one's own potentialities being inferior or superior to those of someone else.

I said that gains and losses of individuality are the fundamental causes of consciousness. Since they are also the conditions for emotion and the objects of emotions of elation and alarm, this tells us that emotion is the primary mode of consciousness.

Emotion is consciousness, first of a difference of individuality, sometimes only of that (we feel disturbed without any perception of what is disturbing us; we feel alarm before identifying its object). But in most cases we are also conscious of what makes the difference of

Consciousness of change in structure is image.

individuality (breaking a dish, meeting a friend). The consciousness of what makes the difference of individuality is consciousness of a change in **structural** conditions. This mode of consciousness is **image**.

Are there images of emotions, or are images of emotions really images of the material changes that elicit those emotions?

The creative factor retains the history of the universe with all the tendencies consequent on changing structure. Similarly, the creative factor as a person's agent of consciousness retains all one's personal history with all the tendencies consequent on its changing structure. Consciousness of that retention is memory of a primary kind. The intensity and vividness of that consciousness depends on the factors just outlined. But part of that consciousness is memory of emotions.

What one can remember one can also imagine. That is, items in one's personal history can be special patterns for potentialities in consciousness.[17] In this way one can imagine emotions — it is imagining the combination of image and tendency that constitutes the emotion.

Feeling is a broader mode of consciousness than emotion, inclusive of emotion. Feeling is consciousness of a comparison of states of individuality, but that individuality need not be one's own. If it is one's own, the feeling is an emotion. If it is not one's own, the feeling is a judgment or an estimation or an evaluation.

❏ For example, if you are comparing arrangements of your furniture to see which is best, these judgments are made by feeling. Some arrangements just look better and feel better than others. But in a case like this you use emotion as well as objective feeling: some arrangements suit you better than others, and you feel better in them.

---

[17]See Appendix A, "Combined Patterns & Wholeness of Similarity".

The maximization of individuality is the dominant tendency of nature and of living individuals. Emotion is consciousness of tendencies affecting oneself. This is obvious in the case of major emotions such as desire and aversion, love and jealousy. The basic appetites are felt as emotions, though it is not customary to call these feelings emotions. Thus, hunger is consciousness of a tendency in oneself to seek food and eat.

These tendencies are variants of the tendency to maximize one's individuality. Thus, when one suffers a loss of individuality, one's tendency to maximize individuality takes the form of seeking to restore one's individuality to its former level. When hungry one seeks to eat; when slighted one seeks to restore one's creditability. When one enjoys a gain of individuality, as when a valued friend pays one a compliment, one's tendency to maximize individuality takes the form of a tendency to take advantage of the circumstances favourable to one's individuality to seek a further gain. Thus, one follows up the compliment by making friendly conversation and gestures, motivated by a tendency to raise one's creditability still higher with this friend.

Emotions fall into three classes according to their causes. These causes are:

1. gains and losses of one's individuality;

2. gains and losses of potentiality for gains or maintenance of one's individuality (due to successes or failures or changes of fortune);

3. comparisons of one's potentialities for gains or maintenance of one's individuality with those of others.

The second of these is pretty much the same as the first. The *consciousness* of a gain or loss of potentiality for individuality is itself a gain or loss of individuality. The third is the basis of emotions such as smugness and envy, feelings of superiority and inferiority, and of being lucky or unlucky.

An aversion is a loss of individuality elicited by the object of aversion (consciousness of which brings a loss of individuality). The result is a state of alarm or discontentment and a tendency to take action to replace its cause with an alternative that will reverse the loss of individuality. One walks away from the obstreperous person at a party and seeks more attractive company.

Necessary Patterns for These Emotions:

The strength of emotions is partly due to their rootedness in necessary patterns in addition to those that support the tendency to maximize individuality. Each of the three classes of emotion noted above is supported by a particular necessary pattern.

1. The necessary pattern for these emotions is the pattern of the progression of minimal events — states of structure with the consequent tendencies alternating with transitions to augmented states. In a local individual process a state with tendencies is a structure with the empty space in front of it, the empty space constituting the potentiality for extensions of the structure, and the transition to a new state places new matter in that empty space, resulting in the actual extension of the process. **The analogy:** Empty space is not individuated, whereas what occupies space is. Thus, the comparison between empty space and occupied space is analogous to the comparison between a lower and a higher level of individuality. And the succession of empty space followed by its occupation is analogous to a gain of individuality, while the reverse succession is analogous to a loss of individuality. Thus, a state (structure with empty space in front of it) followed by the transition to a new state is analogous to a gain of individuality, while a transition to a new state followed by the consequent state (structure with empty space in front of it) is analogous to a loss of individuality. These progressions are necessary patterns, and their analogies with variations of individuality make the tendency component of the emotion stronger. Then, since the emotion itself is the consciousness of the tendency, the analogies also make the emotion more intense.

2. The necessary patterns for the second class of emotions are these:

    • Realized tendencies, analogous to success, bringing new opportunities.

    • Nullified tendencies (due to the realization of competing tendencies), analogous to failure and the loss of opportunity.

    • Modified tendencies (due to changes elsewhere):

        i. to higher potency, analogous to improved opportunities

        ii. to lower potency, analogous to worsened opportunities

3. The necessary patterns for envy etc. are the two classes of **realized tendencies** and **unrealized tendencies**. These are analogous to success and failure. They are also analogous to higher and lower levels of capability or opportunity, since statistically the higher

potencies are more likely to be realized. Thus, someone who is, say, wealthier and more educated than another compares themselves with that other as having superior capability or opportunity, and the analogy to realized tendencies against unrealized tendencies gives the tendency to act with a high level of self-confidence much greater potency.

Point of View:
The body is the focus of complementation.[18]   The person is the complemented body.   This implies that relationships of the person are relationships with the body. They are primarily relationships with the body and secondarily relationships of the person. The person responds to objects by means of the body.

This implies that the body is the normal point of view of consciousness (the centre of the relationship which is the focussed response). Of course there are mechanistic reasons for this when things are perceived by the bodily senses. Things are seen from the perspective of the eyes for optical reasons. Sounds are heard from the perspective of the head. But consciousness is not passively perceptive; it is active; it includes both perception and volition. We move our body into position for perceptions. And we not only sense things consciously, we also act consciously.

Our conscious experience is of the person using the body as an instrument, adjusting its posture and the focus of the eyes, for instance. This is reflected in language: we say, "My body won't do what I want it to do", or, "You shouldn't abuse your body as you do." The implication is that the body is the tool of the person.

The person is conscious.

Thus, it is the person that is conscious, although the body is the normal point of view of consciousness.

Why must it be the person that is conscious?
Consciousness consists of external relationships with the body that are components of individuality — individuality due to those relationships, therefore not of the body without its external relationships but of the **complemented** body, which is the person.

The body is the point of view.

---

[18]See "Significance of Individuality".

The Timing of Consciousness:

How is our consciousness of an event related to the occurrence of the event? Are they simultaneous, or do we become conscious of the event only after it occurs?

Consciousness is aroused by a gain or loss of the person's individuality.

☐ Suppose the event does constitute a gain or loss of a person's individuality.

☐ Then the person is immediately conscious of that gain or loss — this will be an emotion of elation or alarm.

☐ The image component of consciousness depends on the exclusiveness of its immediate object, the object as responded to.

☐ The object will be the object that caused the change of individuality. Before consciousness includes an image, that object must be identified, i.e., it must be focussed on as the object to be responded to. In other words, supposing the change of individuality to be a loss, the first response is to seek to regain individuality, but the first phase of that is to find what has to be changed in order to do that. This causes a delay in the onset of consciousness of the object (the image).

☐ Therefore, while the intensity of the **emotional** aspect of the state of consciousness occurs with the event, the **vividness** of its **image** aspect is delayed.

      o For example, you hear a loud noise and are immediately alarmed. You turn in the direction of the noise to see what has happened. Only after you have gained sensory information and digested it do you have a vivid image of what has happened and are able to take appropriate action to deal with it.

      o The sensory information may be essentially complete at the beginning, and the delay may be mainly to do with what action to take, as, say, if you drop a dish and break it, and it takes a few seconds to see what you need to do to clean up the mess. In this case one's consciousness of the situation acquires exclusiveness as the processing of information in the brain establishes a coherent relationship with the external situation.

One may have the image of an event **before** it occurs, in the sense of anticipating it. This is characteristic of highly skilled activities where response times are shorter than the neural response time to an unanticipated event, as in musical performance and athletics. In these cases the activity is inherently highly predictable and actually highly predictable because of practice.

Tendencies due to Consciousness:
    This section is about the power of volition. To a naive view, there seems to be something magical about the fact that I can, by merely willing it, make my body move in a radically different way from what it would otherwise do. Standard physics and the present account agree on many points, including this: that particles have their own dynamics. And where particles go, the gross bodies they belong to must also go. Conversely, where gross bodies go, their particles must go. How is it, then, that volition can turn the body and all its particles from their courses into a very different one? The materialist view is that volition is something that happens in the brain, and the rest is a matter of control and amplification. However, that view takes no account of transcendence and consciousness. How is it that volition can turn the particles in the brain from their courses to different ones?

☐   The creative factor's effectuation of my conscious response to an object is a response **to my response** as well as being included in the creative factor's response **to the entire universe**.

☐   In my consciousness there are potentialities and patterns and similarities between them, with resulting tendencies, just as there are in the universe.

☐   The similarities and patterns of which I am conscious are similarities and patterns in the universe as well as in my consciousness. They are not isolated from the tendencies in the universe.

☐   Therefore, to take account of all the tendencies affecting me, another term is needed in the formula: similarity x prevalence.

Total tendency =
tendency due to the universe +
tendency due to consciousness =
(similarity in the universe x prevalence in the universe) +
(similarity in consciousness x prevalence in consciousness).

☐   The similarities are the same in the universe and in my consciousness.

☐   But my state of consciousness is minuscule compared with the universe, so that patterns generally have much greater prevalence in consciousness than in the universe. This is especially true of patterns that are peculiar to my consciousness, such as events in my past or my own thoughts. Necessary patterns and highly prevalent patterns such as common particles may have much the same prevalence in consciousness as in the universe.

☐ Therefore, the second term in the expanded formula is generally much greater than the first term, and especially for patterns peculiar to my consciousness. This is the

Tendencies due to consciousness are stronger

basic reason for the special power of volition. When the tendencies are combined, the tendency due to consciousness dominates the sum.

But what about the consistency of the power of volition with the dynamics of particles?

☐ Both physics and the present account say that events at the level of particles are not strictly deterministic. In the present account, there are always many potentialities, locally as well as globally, and the creative factor

than tendencies due to the universe.

selects which of these will be realized. For example, the exact position of a new particle (or particle-state) is selected from an infinity of possible positions in the space immediately in front of the particle-process.

☐ Then the relation between particle-processes and the process of the human body is

Slight bend in particle-processes = sharp bend in body movement.

like the relation between the individual wires in a heavy cable and the cable. A solid rod could not bend in the way that a cable of the same diameter can without being permanently bent. But the individual wires only need a very slight curvature relative to their diameter for the cable to bend as it needs to do. Similarly, particle-processes only need to deviate very slightly from what their courses would be to accommodate the motions of the human body. This deviation would not violate the physics of particles.

☐ In the present account, tendencies at many spatial-temporal scales combine to give a total or net tendency for the next phase of a particle-process. Among these tendencies are the tendencies due to consciousness, and these usually dominate sufficiently to produce the willed motions of the body.

Reasons:

One's reasons for a volition are the patterns of which one is conscious and that are similar to that potentiality. These are "special patterns"[19], and if the reasons are cogent, similarity of an extendible process to them makes it also similar to some very prevalent patterns, especially necessary patterns. For example, an attitude of generous love towards a person gives the extendible process (the generous person) similarity to the transcendent relationships Creation and Beneficence as well as the biological pattern of care of the young, which defines the social animals. One is conscious of having that attitude and takes it as a reason for generous actions. And the combination of that pattern with the necessary patterns gives one a strong conscious tendency to take such actions. In other

Reasons are patterns in consciousness

words, the reasons are more convincing because they are supported by patterns in the foundations of nature. One may not be conscious of those patterns, but one has a feeling that the reasons are not mere personal likes or dislikes.

But what about intellectual reasons such as Newton's law of gravitation as a factor in a lengthy calculation leading to the launch of a satellite? This is not simple similarity with the decision to go on with the launch. But there is a long background of analogies constituting the meanings of symbols, operations, and so on. And it is this background in the experience of the scientists engaged in the project that links Newton's law with the launch in a relation of similarity — that is, the launch is in accordance with Newton's law.

Convincing reasons are not necessarily good reasons. Good reasons are reasons that base volition on truth. That is to say,

Strong reasons may not be good reasons.

they are in agreement (similarity) with the universe. The universe, of course,

---

[19]See Appendix A, 11. Combined Patterns & Wholeness of Similarity

is the original pattern, other patterns being abstracted from it. Good reasons, then, are patterns in consciousness that combine with the pattern of the universe to give the "prevalence" factor in **similarity x prevalence** a high value. The consciousness of this is a feeling that the reasons "ring true".

Volitions & Acts of Will:

A volition is a potentiality due to consciousness. A potentiality **due to the universe** is a process (a structure) in temporal space with empty space in front of it, that spatially extended process being compared with a particular combination of patterns — the comparison with a particular combination of patterns is what defines a particular potentiality. **In our consciousness**, the spatially extended structure is replaced by an **image** of a spatially extended structure. This is because our consciousness is a response of the creative factor to a particular feature of the universe, in addition to its response to the entire universe. As

Consciousness not a structure

such it does not add a new **structure** to the universe. So our consciousness is not a structure but a special view of structure, change, and tendency already there — an image.

Or rather, it is a series of images, since there are distinctive phases of consciousness, and distinctive phases within distinctive phases (an image of a bus stopping followed by an image of passengers leaving a bus, all within an image of the bus travelling along the street; the image covers a certain area of temporal space, and within that area are many distinctive sub-areas — the details, larger and smaller, of what one sees, hears, thinks, etc.). Unlike particles, these are not separate but only distinctive. Those distinctive sub-areas and properties of them are the patterns in one's consciousness.

A potentiality due to consciousness is an image of a spatially extended process and its similarity to a combination of patterns in one's consciousness. A volition with its reasons is a potentiality due to consciousness. However, not all potentialities due to consciousness are volitions. They also include expectations. The difference between expecting it to rain and deciding to carry an umbrella is that the tendency for it to actually rain is not a tendency due to consciousness, whereas the tendency to carry an umbrella is. But the **expectation** of rain is a tendency due to consciousness. So the expectation

Potentialities due to consciousness

of rain has no significant effect on whether it rains or not. This is why we use different words for expectations and volitions. They are both tendencies due to consciousness, but the outcomes related to them are not both due to consciousness.

A volition is not the same as acting on that volition. Acting on a volition goes beyond one's consciousness and is done by the creative factor in responding to the universe, including one's consciousness. For a volition to effectively lead to its execution, the tendency due to consciousness must dominate the total tendency so that the total tendency is in effect a tendency to carry out that volition. In other words acting on a volition is just the realization of that tendency due to consciousness.

are volitions and expectations.

One may decide to do something before doing it. This is a shift from being conscious of the set of options, to do or not to do, to being conscious of the one potentiality as lacking only the conditions for its realization (such as the arrival of the bus one has decided to board). These conditions will be the reasons for acting on the volition. When they are satisfied (in the normal case) the potency of the potentiality is great enough to ensure its realization.

Carrying out a volition takes time, indeed a vast multitude of minimal events. Most of our volitions call for complicated actions with a number of major phases. If I decide to type a certain sentence, this is deciding to type a certain sequence of words. Actually typing those words is typing each letter in the proper sequence and the words in the proper sequence. Typing one of the letters is itself physically a very complicated compound event.

Throughout the entire action, the volition must be maintained. If it is not, the action is terminated or modified. And of course this is often what happens.

But during the execution of a volition, the volition does not persist strictly unchanged. With every local minimal event, there is a change in the state of consciousness and the existing patterns in consciousness. These alter the tendencies. For example, I undertake to make coffee. Initially, this is only the intention to make coffee, but as I actually begin the operation, that global intention develops into the details of making coffee, and these details are responses to the particular circumstances as they arise, which are pretty much the same as usual, but unique in minute details.

Executing a volition is my act & God's act.

So, is the making of coffee an act of my volition, or is it part of the creative factor's response to the universe? The answer is it is both. Insofar as my volitions to perform the details are tendencies that are realized, it is my act of volition, but most of the details of what my body does and how it affects my environment are not acts of my volition but actions of the creative factor in response to the universe.

A difficulty: A tendency, whether due to consciousness or not, is realized by the creative factor, not by the person. How, then, can it be an act of the person's will? **Answer:** The creative factor realizes the total tendency, which includes the tendency due to the universe and the tendency due to consciousness. In responding to the tendency due to consciousness, the creative factor is acting as the person's will. Therefore, insofar as the total tendency is a tendency due to consciousness, its realization is an act of the person's will.

Another difficulty: How is it possible for me to control those actions of the creative factor that are not acts of my volition? The answer is that one learns in the first years of childhood the basics of cooperating with nature,

Control of volitional action is cooperating with nature.

and one develops that skill in the course of one's life. When we try to control nature without cooperating with it, it does something other than what we intend.

It is the same with scientific technology. We talk of conquering nature, but successful technology is successful because we have learned how to **initiate** natural processes that proceed not in obedience to our choices but according to a natural process that we have predicted. It is said of agriculture, "We sow and we till, but God gives the increase." The same is true of technology.

Foreground & Background:

A state of consciousness has exclusiveness, and exclusiveness has degrees, it is not all-or-none. Accordingly, one is not simply conscious or unconscious but conscious to one degree or another, and as we have seen, differently with respect to intensity and vividness. One is always conscious to a degree, because one is always sensitive to one's local environment in a way in which one is not sensitive to the rest of the universe, even in deep sleep or under deep anaesthesia. And one's individuality is always undergoing variations, even if slight. So the conditions for consciousness are always satisfied to a degree.

This means that what we normally call a state of consciousness is really a foreground of a perpetual background state of consciousness of low intensity and vividness. In theoretical terms, the creative factor's consciousness of the person's selective response to an object fades off into the creative factor's response to the person as part of its response to the universe.

An important implication of this is that we are not trapped within our consciousness in the way that has been commonly supposed under the influence of Descartes' philosophy. The creative factor's consciousness of the universe including ourselves is primary, and our selectively focussed consciousness is a modification of it. We are first of all a part of the universe and secondarily focussed on some part of it.

Then there are normally foregrounds within that foreground state of consciousness. For example, I look at the screen of my computer, but I also see the room around. My consciousness of the screen has greater vividness and intensity than my consciousness of the room around. Then on that screen I am looking at the words I am typing. My consciousness of these has more vividness and intensity than my consciousness of the background screen.

☐ The vividness of consciousness is due to the exclusiveness of the response — of the object as responded to. So the contrast of vividness that distinguishes foreground from background is a difference of exclusiveness.

☐ Then, as one's attention is drawn to an object as foreground, the occurrence of that response is a gain of individuality, and that gain gives intensity to one's consciousness of that object.

Choosing from Options:

A volition is a potentiality due to consciousness. A choice from a set of options is also a volition and a potentiality due to consciousness. The options are potentialities of which one is conscious, and to the degree that one is inclined to choose them they are all potentialities due to consciousness. But one is also thinking of the set as the set from which one is to choose (if the options are to buy a Bentley or to buy a Jaguar, one is conscious of that set of options and of the higher-order options of choosing from that set or not, that is, not buying either). So there are two levels of volition: there is the volition to choose from the set, and there is a choice of one option from the set.

Each of these volitions is a potentiality due to consciousness, and each makes its contribution to the tendency of the choice — to choose is to choose from the set, and to choose from the set is to will the set and to will the choice from the set. Therefore, these potencies add up to make the potency of the choice itself.

Total tendency =
tendency due to the universe +
tendency of the options +
tendency of the choice from the options.

This implies that the power of choice is still greater than the power of volition. If you have not only consciously willed something but also willed it in conscious preference to alternatives, the tendency for it to be acted upon is greater than if you had not willed it in conscious preference to alternatives. The

Choice from options is more powerful than mere volition.

conscious preference to alternatives counteracts the tendencies of those alternatives due to the universe (if they are incompatible), which without that consideration of alternatives might have prevailed over the competing volition.

Deliberation:

We can decide among options without executing the chosen option, and we can consider options without deciding amongst them. What is happening here, in terms of causality by patterns?

I said above that to decide to do something before doing it is a shift from being conscious of the set of options (to do or not to do) to being conscious of the one potentiality as lacking only the conditions for its realization. But those conditions may be no more than taking action on what one only intended to do sooner or later. Deciding to do something later (which could just as well be done immediately) is labelling the image of doing it with an indication that it is not to be done now. We do this linguistically, with phrases such as "I'll do that later."

When we decide among options without executing the chosen option, we label the other options with phrases such as "No, I'll do X instead." These phrases are then included in the images of the options. **But more importantly**, we label the rejected options with the image of the chosen option as that to be done instead. The resulting image is an image of a nullified potentiality, unrealizable due to the realization of an incompatible alternative.

Now, the class of all nullified potentialities is a necessary pattern, since each minimal event involves realizing one potentiality and nullifying some others. Therefore, labelling the images in the above way has the effect of raising the potency of those options, because of similarity to the necessary pattern. **However, those options have been redefined so as to reduce all the options to the one chosen.** The consequence is that it is the potency of **that one** that is raised by the similarity of the others to this necessary pattern.

When one considers options with the intention of delaying a decision until one has adequately determined their merits, this also involves labelling the options with an image of one's body not being put into action with respect to that issue. One also labels them linguistically as "to be thought about" or something equivalent.

Considering options without deciding is a matter of manipulating potentialities and the patterns in consciousness and the similarities between them — the reasons supporting the respective options. In consciousness the creative factor is acting as the person's will, not as the will of the universe. So, when an option is altered so as to increase its similarity to patterns, this is an act of the person, and it is appropriate to speak of manipulating the options and their reasons. Most deliberation is cursory and dominated by non-rational emotion. But there are rational emotions too, and rational deliberation (seeking to formulate the most potent options and determine their potencies when all relevant patterns are included) is as much driven by emotion as any other activity. The emotions are familiar — curiosity, doubt, conviction, a sense of mismatch, a sense of something missing. These are the emotions of gains and losses of individuality **when focussing attention on particular options and their supporting patterns** rather than on the interests to be served by those options.

To be satisfied that one has adequately determined the merits of the options is to feel no loss of individuality when they and their reasons are made the foreground of consciousness. At that point one may or may not choose one of them and label the others as nullified by it. And one may or may not re-label the chosen one as "to be acted on". These acts come under the non-determinism of the creative factor's actions in selecting potentialities for realization. And when the total tendency is dominated by tendencies due to consciousness, that non-determinism is more stark than for tendencies due to the universe, because of the paucity of alternative potentialities.

I have been talking about options as distinctive foregrounds of a state of consciousness. But we sometimes think about options that are continuously distributed in space. This brings us to the topic of the continuity of consciousness.

The Continuity of Consciousness:

A state of consciousness is not a second layer of **structure** superimposed on the structure created according to similarity to patterns in the universe. Rather, it is a localized second layer of the creative factor's **consciousness** of that same structure.

❑   If individual consciousness were a structure superimposed on that primary structure, it would be structurally related to it and they would constitute just one structure.   In that case individual consciousness would be part of the creative factor's consciousness of the universe rather than specifically of the individual's response to an object. Therefore, individual consciousness is not a structure.   If it had discrete parts, it would not be a structure but a number of states of consciousness separated by unconsciousness.   Therefore, the question is about any one of these.   It remains, then, that **a single state of individual consciousness is continuous.**

Nevertheless, there can be something like structure embedded in a state of consciousness, in the form of several foregrounds separated by the common background.   This is still not real structure, since the foregrounds are only distinctive, not discrete, and their separation by background is imperfect.

The significance of the continuity of our consciousness is that it enables us to see as continuous what is really discrete in its fine details, such as a painted wall. On the scale of our conscious perceptions and actions, such a surface is effectively continuous and is most accurately perceived as such. If a state of consciousness had discrete parts, we would be conscious of their discreteness (since it is a state of consciousness), and we would be unable to see a painted wall as a continuous surface.

Consciousness is continuous.

For some purposes of formulating options and making choices, it is important to see it as continuous. Say you are going to hang a picture on your wall, and you want to find the best location for it. It is important not to see the wall as made up of discrete parts, since that would severely limit the sense of what the possible locations for the picture are. They should be perceived as continuously distributed over the wall.

Seeing structure as continuous.

Thus, the options for choice in a case like this form a continuous distribution.   Their potencies are also perceived as forming a continuous distribution. So you look at the wall and see certain spots as the most likely locations for the picture. Then you have someone hold the picture up in those locations, and you get a revised perception of the distribution of potencies.

These are total potencies, due to the universe and due to consciousness. Those due to consciousness may be supported by a certain amount of reasoning about proportions and colours, but both those due to the universe and those due to consciousness are perceived by feelings, and it is those feelings that are decisive. This is characteristic of the arts. When artists, whether in the static or the live arts, try to create art on the basis of reasoning or calculation alone, as, for example, resorting to randomness as if it were equivalent to creativity, the result does not strike naive viewers or listeners as art. I think no one in the theatrical arts has ever doubted the absolute dependence of those arts on the criterion of feeling. You know it's not right until it feels right.

Objectivity:

The ideal of reason is that decisions should be made on the basis of truth, all relevant truth. And the divine attribute of Truth shows us what is meant by "truth", ideally, seeing things exactly as they are.

How to see things as they are rather than through the lens of one's emotions? That question is misleading in that it presupposes that to see things as they are and to think rationally in an ideal sense is to be free of emotions. As I said above, there are also emotions of reason, such as doubt and conviction. But these emotions are peculiar in that they are not due to comparisons involving one's individuality as a person, only one's individuality as an inquirer.

Some subject-matters make it easy to leave one's personal individuality behind and be only an inquirer, such as mathematics, the content of which does not affect one's personal individuality, though achievement or failure in it may do so profoundly. But it is with regard to our vital interests — things that affect our individuality as a person — that it would be most beneficial to be able to follow the ideal of reason.

And this is possible because of the possibility of creating special foregrounds of consciousness. The original and normal point of view of consciousness is the body, but imaginary points of view are possible, so long as one has the conceptual equipment to formulate them. Such imaginary points of view are represented by foregrounds of consciousness.

In particular, one can imagine an ideal inquirer who is reasoning about one's interests. They are not the inquirer's interests, and therefore the inquirer is not swayed by the emotions that would distort one's own judgment. This inquirer is fictional, of course, and therefore only does what one imagines him or her to do.

A point of view devoid of one's personal interests.

But the fiction of not having one's interests makes it possible to imagine how such a person would reason about one's interests. Variants of this fiction may be just as effective. For example, one can imagine oneself at a point outside one's body, viewing oneself as a person from a disinterested point of view.

This possibility, of course, depends on the background of a culture that has seen reason as an ideal and cultivated it in at least some subject-matters, such as mathematics and science.

The word "objectivity" is appropriate for this technique, since the effect is to make one's interests objects rather than forces moving one in the direction of what would immediately and apparently bring a gain of individuality.

But as valuable as such a technique is, it does not magically make us decide issues on the basis of objectively considering how to pursue our real interests. The reason is that practical decisions must be made at the first-order level of consciousness. The second-order level of an artificial point of view can only provide the information for such a decision. Reason determines action only to the extent that one chooses that it shall do so. One may still choose on the basis of first-order emotions.

Truth in Practical Contexts:
The transcendent relationship of Truth is the ideal that inspires truth-seeking and affects our conscience about telling the truth. But as a practical matter we can only achieve an analogue of this ideal of Truth, since our consciousness of an object (in contrast with the creative factor's consciousness of it) is not the object itself but the object in relation to the person through the person's response to it.

The practical ideal is that our concepts should be derived from their real objects, not from our preferences or preconceptions or what appears to be socially advantageous. What this amounts to in terms of causality by patterns is that the real object (the object as it is in the universe rather than in consciousness) should be the effective pattern for the concept.

A variant of this is that theories should be tested by observation, not observation by theory. But we often find that observations are declared illusory or fraudulent on the ground that accepted theory implies their impossibility. This is taken to be scientific, but it really violates the most fundamental principle of science, which is the primacy of experience.

To say that the real object should be the effective pattern for the concept is the same as to say that the tendency due to consciousness that gives rise to

> **The object should be the pattern for the concept.**

the concept should be the same as if it were a tendency due to the universe. In other words, the pattern for the concept should be the object as it is in the universe rather than as it is in consciousness, which may be distorted by first-order emotions. Truth here applies to the creative factor's comparison of potentialities with patterns in the universe. In consciousness the creative factor is reduced to the scope of human consciousness, and comparisons are with the patterns in consciousness. Concepts are formed, or at least completed, in consciousness. So the problem, if one is devoted to truth, is how to transcend the scope of consciousness and get at the object as it is in the universe. The best solution we have is, on the one hand to cultivate objectivity and on the other hand to extend the scope of consciousness to encompass a fuller consciousness of the object as it is in the universe.

Self-Deception & Distraction:

Say there is an event in one's experience that is either distressing or alarming (a distressing event might be the death of a loved one; an alarming event might be a wrong deed one has committed, the memory of which defines one as having betrayed one's moral community). This is a loss of individuality and elicits a tendency to restore the lost individuality. But the event cannot be undone. The nearest to that that can be done is to remove the event from one's consciousness, at least to a degree.

This cannot be done by some kind of negative attention to the event. Attention, whether favourable or unfavourable, is always positive and makes consciousness more vivid and intense. The tendency is to direct attention elsewhere and follow the opportunities available, that is, the potentialities that promise gains or losses of one's individuality. One of these is to deny or modify the fact, and when we find ourselves embarrassed by what we have said or done, we tend to focus attention on an interpretation of it that is more favourable to ourselves (or even an outright denial). The other recourse is to shift attention to a different subject matter — what has been called "displacement behaviour" (a squirrel who is too cautious to come and take the nut may become very attentive to its lice).

Human ingenuity over the centuries has been largely exercised on devices of self-deception. A good deal of religion consists of ways of convincing oneself either that the world is safe or that there is compensation available for its dangers. A good deal of deliberating and theorizing about ethics consists of ways of justifying the compromise of acknowledged moral principles. In the cultural developments of the Twentieth Century, it seems to me that a good deal of artistic ingenuity has been spent on taking the sting out of ethics; in contrast with the tradition of moral stories in the Nineteenth Century, Twentieth Century fiction focussed on the problematic character of moral situations and then more and more turned to an essentially amoral kind of narrative that carries the message (perhaps not overtly intended) that ethics is not objectively real.

Distraction, while not overtly self-deceptive, can serve the same purpose. Much of what has been done in the respectable portion of civilized life has been, to any moderately responsible view, morally compromised if not outrightly immoral. Much of what we take pride in is destructive of our habitat. No one with an awareness of ethics would attempt to justify the destruction of our habitat, though they might argue that the degree of destruction is not serious. But we have avoided the need for such justification by keeping very busy at those same pursuits. The bustle of business as usual provides an effective distraction from thinking about global and long-term consequences, keeping our conscience innocently uninformed.

"Higher" States of Consciousness and Complexity:

There are more and less complex states of consciousness, according to the structure of foregrounds and backgrounds. But if "higher" means of a more spiritual nature, it is likely to be less complex than "lower" forms of consciousness. For example, someone engaged in the deception both of others and of themselves is likely to have quite complex states of consciousness in terms of points of view and foregrounds and backgrounds.

Attitudes:

This book is proposing an emphasis on attitudes rather than problems. What does this mean? What is an attitude?

- ❏ Attitudes are favourable or unfavourable, sympathetic or unsympathetic, toward their objects.
- ❏ One can adopt an attitude; one can decide to cultivate a different attitude from what one has had.

- ❏ For example, one may have racist feelings, and one may decide that they are wrong and adopt a non-racist attitude, thus intending to cultivate feelings favourable to the race in question
- ❏ Thus, an attitude is something one can choose.
- ❏ Like a policy, an attitude tends to lead to certain kinds of actions. But unlike a policy, an attitude does not specify actions. Instead, it specifies feelings and the images that elicit those feelings.

Putting these points together, we see that **an attitude is an intention to have feelings of a certain kind toward a certain object or class of objects.**

- ❏ The objects need not be persons. One may disapprove of the new architecture one sees downtown and adopt a disapproving attitude towards it. In that case, one intends to dislike buildings of that sort.

How is it possible to have an intention to have feelings of a particular kind? The tendency component of a feeling is consequent on the state of structure and its history, not a possible object of effective volition.

❑   As was noted above,[20] one can imagine an emotion. To intend to have an emotion of a particular kind, one imagines the emotion & forms the volition to have such emotions, that is, such a combination of image and tendency when presented with the causes of such images. The volition effects the images, and the images elicit the emotions.

❑   One can will to think of people of other races as practically the same as people of one's own race so far as innate capabilities and proclivities go and therefore to feel about them in the same way that one feels about those of one's own race.

Attitudes are more powerful than policies in determining behaviour. This is because action is the realization of tendencies.

❑   Attitudes cultivate feelings, and feelings have a component of tendency favourable or unfavourable, sympathetic or unsympathetic towards the object.

❑   These tendencies lead one to act in ways that are functional or counter-functional toward the object.

❑   Policies, however, do not have a tendency component (unless they express attitudes). Policies are pure image, and those images, if combined with attitudes contrary to those policies, generate tendencies contrary to the policies.

Thus, if attitudes are inconsistent with policies, it is attitudes that dominate action.

Is Consciousness Restricted to the Living?

A question of keen interest to most of us is whether there is anything like life after death. Of course, life, literally, after life has ceased would be a contradiction. But what people are interested in is whether there is any conscious experience after death.

All that one has been in life continues to exist in the past and is, and will always be, a potentially effective pattern for future lives.[21] What does this imply as regards consciousness?

---

[20]See "Emotions & Feelings".

[21]See Appendix A, 1. The Nature of Change, and 9. Causality by Patterns.

❑ Consciousness occurs when two conditions are satisfied:[22]

❑ The person undergoes a gain or a loss of individuality.

❑ The person responds to the source or apparent source of that gain or loss in a way that is concentrated **exclusively** on it, leaving other objects out.

Now suppose that a dead person is an effective pattern for someone living, that is, the example of the dead person's life effectively shapes the living person's life as a whole, say with a gain of individuality. The significance of "as a whole" is that the effect is focussed on the person **as whole and distinctive.**

❑ This is a relationship between the dead person and the living person **as a whole**, and it is an active relationship, that is, the dead person is an active cause affecting the life of the living person — active through the action of the creative factor mediating the relationship of influence.

❑ Notice that action does not imply that the agent undergoes any change. The example that proves this is the creative factor itself, which is the active element of the universe but undergoes no change. In the present case, the dead person does undergo some change, namely by gaining a new relationship. But it is not that change that makes it an active cause.

Is the gaining of this new relationship by the dead person a gain or loss of individuality?

❑ The occurrence of the relationship is an increase of similarity between the dead and the living.

❑ The relationship is a comparison made by the creative factor. As such it comprises the properties of each relatum compared, that is, the creative factor's consciousness of the comparison includes

---

[22]See "How does the creative factor's consciousness become an individual person's consciousness?" earlier in "Consciousness, Choice, & Reasoning".

consciousness of the properties compared. This includes the gain of individuality of the living (which was our assumption).

❑ That gain is therefore a gain to the dead due to acquiring the relationship. This then satisfies one of the conditions for the dead to be conscious of the living.

Is this new relationship of the dead person an exclusive response?

❑ The relationship is one of active causation, therefore a response on the part of the dead to the living. That it is only a comparison made by the creative factor does not contradict this, since the creative factor effectuates every action.

❑ And the assumption was that the effect was on the living person **as a whole**, therefore as whole and distinctive, therefore separating it from other things, therefore exclusive.

❑ Therefore, it is a response that is concentrated **exclusively** on the living person, leaving other objects out. This satisfies the second condition for the dead to be conscious of the living.

Therefore, the dead person is conscious of its influence on the living.

12 ETHICS & SELF-VALIDATION

Ethics Is Peculiar to the Social Animals:
These species give prolonged and intimate care to their young. The young need that care, and the natural providers (sisters in the case of the social insects, otherwise mothers and/or fathers) have an instinctive need to provide it. To the degree that the care of the young is both prolonged and intimate, the species has the character of a social species, which is the same as to say that it has moral communities, communities in which individuals are dependent on one another economically and emotionally. By contrast, a turtle, for example, which is on its own as soon as it hatches, has no need for love, and turtles have no moral communities. Their only social life is mating. Similarly, turtles do not become pets. People may think they have a turtle as a pet, but to the turtle it is only an imprisonment, and at every opportunity it will run away.

The Parental Instinct:
The child's individuality is important to the parent in the same way as the parent's own individuality is important to herself, as if it were a basic tendency of nature. Just as living individuals have an instinctive compulsion to protect and further their own individuality, so the parent in whom the parental instinct is functioning has an instinctive compulsion to protect and further the individuality of the child. An aspect of the importance of the child's individuality to the parent is gratitude for the existence and developing individuality of the child and a need for the child's presence and vivacity. (A need for the child's presence is a dependence of the parent's individuality on the presence of the child — a gain of the parent's individuality due to the presence of the child and a loss of the parent's individuality when deprived of

the presence of the child.) The parental instinct is the original form of love and the pattern for other forms of love.

Does the Parental Instinct Contradict Basic Nature?

If the dominant tendency of nature and of each living individual is to maximize its individuality opportunistically, how is it possible to shift that tendency to another individual, "**as if** it were a basic tendency of nature". The answer must be that the parental constitution is such that gains or losses in the individuality of the child cause gains or losses in the parent as well. And this is implied in saying "a gain of the parent's individuality due to the presence of the child and a loss of the parent's individuality when deprived of the presence of the child". This is possible because a gain or loss in the individuality of the parent's **relationship** with the child is a gain or loss in the parent's individuality, and external relationships primarily define one's individuality as a whole. It does not follow from this that the parent cares for the child **in order to** gain individuality herself. Of course that can be the case. But the parental instinct is not an intention, not a conceptual factor, and therefore its conscious manifestation is not an intention in order to gain individuality for the parent.

There is also the fact that in the pattern of biological parenthood in mammals there is a partial identity between parent and child, since the child begins as part of the parent and becomes a separate individual as a distinctive phase of the same larger process. This gives the parent an ambiguous consciousness of the child as both a part of herself and also a separate individual. The latter image properly takes precedence over the former, since it represents the present circumstance. But parents are sometimes confused and fail to cherish the child's individuality because of thinking of it as a part of themselves.

Properties of the Parental Instinct:

Gratitude, generosity, carefulness, and dependability: (1) **Gratitude** as just indicated. (2) **Generosity**: The parental instinct is unconditional; it does not depend on any particular response from the child, other than continued life. Thus, it is a generous impulse to care for the child. (3) **Carefulness**: The parent's concern is to further the individuality of the child. This concern extends to the details of caring for the child, so that the parent's impulse is to care for the child carefully. (4) **Dependability**: For the same reason, the parent's concern is constant and attentive to the continuing needs of the child, hence dependability is a property of the parental instinct. These are the properties of love, which has the two aspects of desire for and pleasure in the presence of the loved one in a state of high vivacity, and desire for and pleasure in contributing to such a state.

How the Parental Instinct Works:

The way in which one's importance to oneself works is this: one's basic tendency is to follow the gradient of individuality up its steepest slope, which is to maximize vivacity. To attach the same kind of importance to another is to tend to do what is apparently conducive to maximizing their vivacity. The mechanisms of the body are adapted for producing offspring that need parental care as well as for providing such care (such as the mother's production of milk). In addition, the bodily makeup of the parent and her external relationships are shaped by the pattern of parental care in the social species. This similarity gives potentialities for taking care of the young high potency. And in the consciousness of the parent, images of the offspring and of its vivacity and the parent's relationship to the offspring have close similarity to that pattern. This evokes a representation of a gain of individuality in the parent because of the presence of the offspring in a state of high vivacity. That consciousness is itself a gain of individuality for the parent. On the other side of that coin, images of the offspring in a state of low vivacity evoke representations of alarm and a tendency to take corrective action. Thus, although the parent's generosity is not **conditional** on gains in the parent's individuality, the parent does experience gains of individuality because of love. Love, though other-directed, not self-directed, is beneficial to the one who loves.

Love, Sex, & Romance:

The theory of causality by patterns makes it possible to disentangle these central realities of human life that have been the cause, not only of much joy, but also of much distress. And the confused conceptions of how these things are related have deprived people of some of the potentially greatest satisfactions of life. Nowhere is the entanglement of these concepts more

Love and sex follow very different patterns.

evident that in the very different meanings attached to the word "love".

Sexual passion and love (in the sense that implies generosity and care) have very different patterns behind the powerful passions that come under these names.

Sexual passion derives from the very large class of exchanges of material between living individuals — from exchanges of genetic material between bacteria to the consumption of one life by another as food, to the blossoming of plants to attract pollinating insects, to all varieties of copulation. In the vast majority of instances of this large class there is no trace of love in the sense of concern for the welfare of the other. And the metaphors and expressions people use to express sexual passion are largely suggestive of attack, violence, predation, and consumption as food — snarls, bites, "a tasty morsel", and the like. Sexual passion, no doubt, is nature's way of ensuring the propagation of the species, but it is not nature's way of making life enjoyable, unless, of course, it is guided by love. The popular view to the contrary is based on confusing desire with ensuing pleasure. While intense sexual desire may be almost universal in young adults, real pleasure in the consummation of that desire is by no means universal.

Love, by contrast, derives from the class of care of the young that characterizes the social animals. The young of these species need to be not only provided with the bare necessities of life but also given prolonged and intimate care — affectionate intimacy. They need to be given expressions of assurance of their importance to those who care for them. And the providers have an instinctive need for an intimate relationship with the young and an instinctive concern for the well being of the young. This parental instinct and the relationships of love that exist between providers and young constitute the pattern for love. And this is reflected in the metaphors and expressions used to express love, such as "baby" and various crooning vocalizations suggestive of a lullaby.

Romantic love combines sexual passion with love rooted in the parental instinct. As such it is rooted in the entire pattern of parenthood, from the pattern of mere procreation to that of the loving care of the offspring. To think of being in love as having no connection with parenthood is to misread the emotions of romantic love. It is true that being in love does not morally commit one to having children or even wishing to have them, but the emotions of being in love are nonetheless rooted in that entire pattern of parenthood. Consequently, for example, an expectation of enduring loyalty is inherent in being in love, especially on the woman's part. The parties may agree that the relationship can be terminated amicably and comfortably, but nature is not a party to this understanding. Popular songs about ended love affairs tell nature's version of the story.

Historically, romantic love has been an important factor in improving the lot of girls and women and shifting the emphasis of culture from warlike to peaceful ideals — from masculine preoccupations to feminine preoccupations. From the Middle Ages to the Nineteenth Century, tales in which marriage for love (romantic love) contends against marriage for family connections dominated fictional literature and undoubtedly had a good deal to do with liberating girls from the status of merchandise in marriage arrangements.

The patterns in which sexual passion and love are rooted are, as I said, very different and even contrary to each other. Consequently, parents engaged in caring for children tend either to give sexual relations less importance than they did or to treat them as less passionate and more as an expression of love, in other words to transform their rootedness into that of love.

Genuine love is a relationship that need have no sexual involvement at all, as between "just friends". There are many opportunities for the enjoyment of love in friendship, provided these things are not confused. But the myth of romantic love **as the paradigm of love** has systematically confused them.

What binds a human community, and what binds individuals in an enjoyable relationship, is the generalization of the love between parent and child. Without that element of sociable love, a community is only an economic arrangement, a "marriage of convenience" that is only as durable as the advantage that individuals find in it, and the same for friendship.

When one realizes that love is the essential factor in a community, that realization opens up opportunities for enjoyment. Love is enjoyable, provided it is

Love is the essence of a community.

not distorted by false expectations and false notions of propriety or of what is natural — such as that love implies marriage or that love between persons of the same sex is unnatural and perverted. Love without sex is just as delightful as love with sex and far less hazardous. And the more broadly one's attitude of love is spread the more enjoyable one's life can be.

People come to realize that love is the essential factor in a community in times of catastrophe, as New Yorkers have experienced just now (September 2001). How unfortunate that it takes a catastrophe to bring that truth home!

The Defining Property of a Moral Community:

Members who are full participants in a moral community **feel the individuality of other members to be important to them in the same way that their own individuality is important to them,** as if it were a basic tendency of nature (though the degree of importance may be quite different). Two points are worth dwelling on in this statement. One is that it is the **individualities** of other members that are felt to be important in this way when sociable love is genuine. Other persons may be important to one in various ways; the ethical way is a need for and a cherishing of their individualities, their wholeness and distinctiveness, their welfare and their uniqueness. That need is common to every social animal, but the individual may not appreciate that the need is for the **individuality** of the other, still less cherish that individuality. The other is the importance of this phrase **"in the same way that their own individuality is important to them"**. The individualities of those who are closest to us, especially our children, may be *more* important to us than our own, while the individualities of remote members of our moral community may be much *less* important to us than our own. But in all these cases, insofar as we are full participants in a moral community, they have the *same kind* of importance to us as our own individuality, **as if it were a basic tendency of nature.** That is, we are spontaneously pleased at gains of their individualities and distressed at losses and feel a certain compulsion to assist them in trouble and encourage them in prosperity (perhaps not strong enough to move us to overt action).

This is true of arbitrarily defined communities such as clubs as well as natural ones based on geographical proximity and mutual economic dependence. A club may be for the express purpose of playing bridge, but its effectiveness depends on the mutual importance of members' individualities. The benefit received is positive vivacity. **Thus, the parental instinct is also the defining property of a moral community**. The importance that members have for one another is derived from the intimacy and affection between parent and child, but also from the economic aspect of care for the child. Members of a natural moral community are dependent on one another for the necessities of life as well as for communal feeling.

The First Social Species:

Ants are social animals of great antiquity as compared with mammals. But far more ancient are the very first moral communities. I mean the multi-celled organisms. Why do I say these are moral communities?

☐ Biological cells are living individuals, and I have argued that all living individuals have consciousness. It is obvious that cells must react with alarm to some situations in order to live, and the conditions for alarm are also conditions for individual consciousness, so that cells have consciousness.

☐ A multi-celled organism begins as a single cell and grows as that cell divides and its successive offspring divide. Thus, the offspring of that process of division constitute the multi-celled body. The body is to the cells as an organization is to the persons who form it, and the same is true of the body's subsystems.

☐ The cells constituting the body either collaborate functionally to maintain the body and its subsystems, or they fail to do so and a disease condition results.

☐ Since the cells are conscious, if they collaborate functionally, they do so by volition as well as unconsciously, and their volitions have an emotional component. (From a materialist viewpoint, this would seem like wild fantasy, and it would seem that only an organism of the complexity of the human body could have the emotions of morality and ethics. But from the viewpoint of causality by patterns these emotions do not presuppose much complexity at all, that is, in biological terms, where even a living cell is extremely complex as compared with a machine of human invention.)

☐ Either the cells are motivated by sociable love or they are not.

    ☐ If they are, other cells and the body are important to them in the same way as they are to themselves. In this case they will collaborate functionally with respect to one another and the body.

    ☐ If they are not, other cells and the body are not important to them in the same way as they are to themselves. In this case they will not collaborate functionally with respect to one another and the body. Instead, they will function only according to their own importance to themselves.

☐ In other words, the cells of a multi-celled organism have the properties of members of a moral

A multi-celled organism is a moral community.

community, and the body of the organism has the properties of a moral community.

☐ The subsystems of the body may be viewed as the institutions of that moral community.

☐ But the body is more than a moral community; it is also a living individual. As being composed of the cells, it is a moral community, but as being the focus of complementation with its subsystems and with entities and systems external to it, it is the core of a living individual with consciousness and emotions — the focus of the whole person.

☐ The whole person is a member of the moral community, which is its body. And as such it may or may not have sociable love with respect to the other members of that community. Like individual cells, it may collaborate functionally

The whole person is a member of it.

with respect to them and the community (its body). Or, since its body is also the core of itself, it may act functionally with respect to its body in disregard of the other members (the cells). Or, it may act on its own (on behalf of the whole person), functionally with respect to its external relationships in disregard of its body and the cells.

But do these moral communities have the equivalent of prolonged and intimate care of the young?

- ☐ The relationship among neighbouring cells must, I suppose, be described as intimate. And any given cell is throughout its life in such an intimate relationship with other cells.
- ☐ If the cells have sociable love for one another, that prolonged and intimate relationship is one of care. If not, it is not, but the same is true of parents' relationships with their children, which is not always one of prolonged and intimate care. And in both cases, to the degree that prolonged and intimate care fails so does the moral community. And as the **moral** community fails, so does the **economic** welfare of its members.
- ☐ Therefore, the answer to this question seems to be affirmative.

Is this information relevant to bodily health? Can one do anything effective towards cultivating sociable love in the cells of one's body, preventing them from becoming amoral, as in cancer?

- ☐ In relation to other persons, showing sociable love towards them tends to elicit sociable love in return, provided they have a degree of sociable love already.
- ☐ The same principle applies to the cells of one's body. If one shows sociable love towards them, they may be expected to show sociable love in return. This is because, like human persons, they have the emotions of members of a moral community.
- ☐ Emotional responses are intelligent, that is, they are responses to benefit and harm as such, not to conditions of changing structure as such, which may not reliably indicate benefit or harm. Consequently, T-lymphocytes, the "law enforcement" members, if they have love relative to the body, will be pleased or alarmed by what they encounter according to whether it is beneficial or harmful to the body. Apart from mistakes, if they do not do this, they are like police who have become corrupt.
- ☐ Cancer cells, which are the amoral characters among cells, will not respond in this way but will only respond to benefit and harm to themselves, unaffected by benefit or harm to others. They must be treated as enemies. But the healthy cells, which have sociable love, may respond to sociable love by enhanced sociable love, and as a manifestation of that, by attacking any cancer cells that are present.

☐ On the other hand, an attitude of resentment and anger towards one's body when it fails to function fully tends to elicit a similar attitude in the body's cells. Thus, natural though this reaction is, it may be making us sick or aggravating an illness due to other causes.

Some Conjectures on the above Basis: A malignant tumour and a healthy organ such as the heart differ in the following way: The cells of the heart have sociable love for one another and form a successful moral community. Consequently, they have no tendency to migrate away from the heart. Moreover, they have no tendency to become amoral, since it is in their manifest interest to continue in sociable love for one another. The heart does not threaten to metastasize. The cells of a malignant tumour, by contrast, lack sociable love for one another and do not form a moral community. Consequently, the tumour is not like an organ; the cells are detached individuals and have no resistance to migrating.

Cancer cells divide without restraint, whereas cell division of healthy cells is restrained by conditions of functionality. Why? Do amoral cells have an apparent interest in dividing? Yes, for the following reason: When a cell becomes two cells, that cell is in a sense identical with the two product cells. Thus, the apparent benefit from dividing is that to be two rather than only one is more conducive to surviving. However, the same argument does not extend to a second division yielding four cells. The reason is that the cell in the first phase is not connected by its own division to those four cells and will not have a self-definition as being the same as them, which it will do in relation to the immediate product of its own division. Thus, each cell has a motive to divide, but not a motive of a sort that would unite them all as a moral community (a family).

Moral characteristics are not separate from and independent of structural properties. Cells commonly become malignant because of DNA damage, so structural properties can determine moral characteristics. Similarly, a human may suffer brain damage that transforms their moral propensities from those of sociable love to those of resentful malice. Thus, when cells become amoral, this must not be understood as something "psychic" and devoid of material properties. Tendencies are determined by the state of structure and its history.

From the Parental Instinct to a Larger Moral Community:

The parental instinct becomes sociable love.

Human beings are more complicated than single cells, and human communities are more complicated than communities of cells. When a child is treated with good care as to necessities and also with consistent affectionate intimacy, it naturally responds with reciprocal affectionate intimacy. The child's emotion in this response is gratitude — perception of being important to the parent, feeling a gain of individuality, and expressing desire for the individuality of the parent. The underlying dynamic of this is a tendency to support the individuality that supports its (the child's) individuality; the consciousness of that tendency is the emotion of gratitude. As the child grows, if this relationship continues, and the child is given clearly perceptible opportunities to reciprocate in practical ways as well as in shows of affection, it will do so. That this does not happen as commonly as might be supposed is due to the parent's typical ineptitude in providing those opportunities. But in this way, imperfectly, the family develops as a moral community. The parental instinct has been transferred to the child as sociable love.[23] This occurs in part through the child's sensitivity to the parent's emotions, but largely because the relationship between parent and child, although not identical in both directions, is largely the same for both parent and child. Thus, the emotions and habits of the parent are transferred to the child directly through being shared.

How Sociable Love Works:

The child reciprocates the parent's love, and the resulting love for the parent is sociable love with respect to the family as a moral community. As the child is welcomed into larger moral communities and presented with the parent's sociable love, that pattern together with the potentialities of participation in that larger community generate sociable love on the part of the child, that is, desire for and pleasure in the presence of members of that community in a state of high vivacity. The deeper support for that desire and pleasure is similarity of the child's external relationships to the pattern of care of the young in the social species.

Conferring Individuality:

The parent not only supports the spontaneous development of individuality in the child but also **confers** individuality on it. This is first of

Parents & community confer individuality on the child.

---

[23]By "sociable love" I do not mean love of a community but love that is not the parental instinct but of which the parental instinct and the family are the patterns.

all by welcoming the child into the family as a moral community. The child is well aware of its **dependence** on the parent for safety and sustenance. A good parent behaves in ways that assure the child of dependability in providing that safety and sustenance. This is conferring on the child the status of member of the moral community with respect to its economic nature. Then, expressions of the parent's need for the presence of the child and pleasure in it confer on the child the status of member with respect to its presence in the community being desired by and pleasing to another.

The status conferred on a child varies with age. A very young child cannot undertake to contribute to the economic resources of the community. With increasing maturity a child can undertake increasing responsibilities. Just what sort of status is conferred on children of various ages varies with the culture. In almost every case, a child is eager, one may say desperate, to join the community in which it finds itself. Therefore, it eagerly accepts the status conferred on it unless the community appears to be positively destructive of its individuality, even if it is expected to assume greater responsibility than is appropriate.

Individuality is conferred on adults as well as on children. Whenever someone is offered a position of any responsibility, or awarded any honour, this is a conferral of status and of individuality. And of course it may be either accepted or rejected.

But any form of welcoming another into one's moral community is a conferring of membership in that community. Everyday social interactions in which expressions of sociable love are exchanged are mutual conferrals of individuality and membership.

God's Conferral of Existence and Individuality:

We were created as structure by the creative factor, particle by particle. This is the work of the transcendent relationship Creation. And our individuality is the result of the basic tendency of nature to maximize total individuality, which is the transcendent relationship Beneficence. Thus, we can say that God has conferred our existence and our individuality on us.

Other Observations about God:

Creation and Truth are necessary patterns, but Beneficence is only a tendency, though the dominant one. Consequently, God's beneficence and the gift of our individuality are imperfect. If God were a person endowed with

God also confers individuality.

omniscience and omnipotence as represented in traditional theology, that imperfection would be blameworthy, and this, of course, has troubled many believers, unwilling as they are to attribute imperfection to God.   In the present account, God is not powerful in any human sense.   Nor do God's actions include good or evil deeds.   God is affected by tendencies that include those for good and evil deeds, but God's actions are only creations of particles, minimal events of which myriads are needed to make up any humanly significant deed.   God is the slave of nature, but nature imposes only tendencies, not actions; in the creation of particles God is free, so that particle-events have the probabilistic character attributed to them by physics.   In a sense God could be said to know everything, everything that actually exists, which does not include events in the future.   The only sense in which God knows the future is that God is conscious of all tendencies, short- and long-term.

Is God Pleased and Distressed by Our Gains and Losses of Individuality?

The transcendent relationships Creation, Truth, and Beneficence are not only relationships between the creative factor and the universe but also relationships between the creative factor and individual processes. Beneficence in particular is a concrete relationship with each individual process.

☐   A gain in my individuality is a "success" of the transcendent relationship Beneficence in furthering my individuality (a realization of the tendency as a concrete relationship with me).   This is also a gain in the individuality of the concrete relationship itself, and thus a gain in God's individuality.

But does this imply that God is pleased?   Emotions are the consciousness of tendencies affecting one's individuality.

☐   The creative factor is conscious of all that occurs.   Therefore, God also is conscious of all that occurs.   Therefore, God is conscious of any gain in the individuality of the transcendent relationship Beneficence in relation to any given individual process and of the consequent gain in God's individuality.
☐   Therefore, **God is pleased when I experience a gain of individuality, and similarly, distressed when I experience a loss of individuality.**
☐   Therefore, it can be said that **God loves us.**

The Importance of the Transcendent Relationships for Ethics:

The transcendent relationships constitute our complementation with the creative factor.   As such they belong to our unconscious nature.   Since they are patterns for the parental instinct and for ethical attitudes, it follows that ethical attitudes are built in to our instinctive nature.   Here the parental instinct is a special pattern that combines with the transcendent relationships to give a combination of patterns with close match and high prevalence. That match, however, is no closer than the strength of the parental instinct, and that commonly is very weak except in relation to one's children. Consequently, the transcendent relationships do not ensure that strong ethical attitudes are built into our unconscious nature.

Ethics is important not only for the emotional and spiritual welfare of the members of a moral community, but also for their economic welfare and very survival. It is easily observed how crime and failures of rudimentary ethics in business can devastate a community. Consequently, the need for strong and universal ethical attitudes is very great. The transcendent relationships can help to serve this need.

The transcendent relationships — patterns for ethics

But for this to be so they need to be patterns in consciousness as well as in the universe, and their ethical analogues need to be conscious potentialities. (We have seen how the dynamics of consciousness can be more powerful than that of unconsciousness.)[24] This is a matter of culture and education.

A sense of the transcendent relationships, however conceived, and their pre-eminent importance has historically been the foundation of religion, along with a sense of the responsibility for educating children. Part of that responsibility is seen as a need to give the child an experience of the sacredness of the transcendent relationships. For the young child, religious rituals have this effect — rituals in which adults are seen taking something very seriously, something that is not part of everyday pragmatic experience but has some mystery about it.

Is consciousness of the transcendent relationships and their sacredness necessary for an ethical attitude? No, all that is necessary is to have experienced parental love and to have reciprocated it, to have been welcomed into larger communities, and to have been taught the importance of honour. However, consciousness of the transcendent relationships and their sacredness gives one a sense that the ethical attitude is of a piece with the fundamental creative and coherent activity of all reality and its dominant tendency. This gives sociable love and honour a solidity and stability that similarity with biological and social patterns alone does not have. One can have reasons for becoming embittered against life and society, but one cannot

---

[24]See "Tendencies Due to Consciousness" in "Consciousness, Choice, & Reasoning".

have reasons for becoming embittered against God, unless one conceives of God as the ruler of the universe.

The Absolute Importance of Living Individuals:

Living individuals are important to themselves, and some of them are important to others. But are they absolutely important; are they important independently of being important to themselves or to other individuals in temporal space?

☐ The meaning of "they are important to themselves" is that they have a tendency to promote their individuality and have accompanying emotions.

☐ The meaning of "they are important to me" is that I have a tendency to promote their individuality and have accompanying emotions.

☐ By the equivalent criterion, "they are absolutely important" means that there is an absolute tendency to promote their individuality, independently of being important to themselves or to other individuals in temporal space, with accompanying emotions.

☐ There is such an absolute tendency, the dominant tendency of nature (Beneficence), and we have just seen that God has the accompanying emotions.

☐ Therefore, living individuals are absolutely important, independently of being important or not to other living individuals.

Responsibilities, Rights, & Privileges:

Responsibility is the conferral on the person of major external relationships. As such, it is a conferral of the person's individuality as a whole person. Rights and privileges are also conferrals of major external relationships and of the person's individuality as a whole person.

Responsibilities for adults

These two types of conferral follow the patterns of the two sides of the parent-child relationship, as applied to the parent (for responsibility) and as applied to the child (for rights and privileges). As such, they also follow the patterns of the two sides of the transcendent relationships, the active side by

Rights & privileges for children

which the parent is analogous to God, and the passive side, by which the child is analogous to all individual processes. The effect of these analogues on potentialities strengthens the child's sense of entitlement to care and provision and the parent's sense of responsibility.

The other factor affecting the potency of potentialities is whether the conferral is on the adult or on the child. If the conferral matches the pattern, the potency of potentialities is greater than if the match is weaker. For this reason, rights and privileges confer greater individuality on children than on adults, and responsibilities confer greater individuality on adults than on children, with a gradation between these extremes as the child matures. In other words, the pattern of life that has greatest total individuality is that of children enjoying the right to optimum care and privileges of special pleasures, and a transition to enjoying responsibilities as the child becomes an adult.

Just as the rights and privileges are primarily appropriate to children, so responsibilities, whatever form they take, ought to be understood as responsibilities for ensuring that children enjoy their rights and privileges.

Responsibility Is Pleasant:

To have one's individuality as a member of a moral community conferred on one is a major gain in individuality, which is positive vivacity of which one is conscious. Therefore, responsibility is in general pleasant.

Responsibility is pleasant.

Self-validation:

To have membership in a moral community conferred on one and to have accepted it as just described is to be subject to fear of loss of that status, of one's presence no longer being desired, or even of one's economic support by the community being lost. That social fear is the impetus of self-validation — the need to maintain and enhance one's creditability in the community in the eyes of others and in one's own eyes.

Self-validation is fear of loss of creditability.

That fear leads one to form changing self-definitions moment by moment in accordance with opportunistic individuality. The fear of loss of creditability leads one to define oneself

Changing self-definitions.

according to what will at the moment apparently make one creditable. The sustenance is the individuality of self-validation.

These changing individualities are individualities of one's relationships rather than the individuality of the whole person, which changes slowly as new substance is added to the total person.

Causality by Patterns in a Moral Community:

The parent is a pattern for the child through causality by patterns, and not only a pattern but a special pattern in the child's consciousness.[25] The child needs to be important to its providers, and this amounts to a need to belong to the moral community that they constitute. The habits and attitudes of the providers are the patterns of participation in that community, and the child's desire to participate makes the potentiality of participating similar to those patterns. That similarity is increased as the child absorbs the parent's habits, emotional responses, and attitudes. Thus, the parent's influence on the child through a shared relationship is increased as the child sees the parent as setting the standard of participation in the moral community.

People are patterns for one another.

The emotions of comparing oneself with others[26] are involved in this dynamic as well as the emotions of variations of individuality. If one sees oneself as not measuring up to the standard of moral participation set by those one sees as creditable members of the moral community, one is distressed and has a tendency to seek to bring one's attitude and conduct up to that standard. But the same dynamic works in the other direction as well. One feels justified if one is no worse than those one sees as creditable members of the moral community. In this way the moral example one sets influences others to be as good as oneself, but also to be no better than oneself.

Another way in which this works is this: One disapproves of certain classes of people, defined by certain moral characteristics. One intends to avoid those characteristics. In this case one forms potentialities of attitude and conduct that are morally superior to those disapproved characteristics. In this way one feels superior in one's intention, and that feeling is also a gain of individuality. Whether that intention is ever carried out or not distinguishes honour from self-validation by appearances.

---

[25]See Appendix A, 11, "Combined Patterns & Wholeness of Similarity".
[26]See "Emotion & Feeling" in "Consciousness, Choice, & Reasoning".

We see, then, that emotions of comparing oneself with others may have either good or ill tendencies.

The Two Moral Motives:

One's motivation as a member of a moral community has these two aspects: love and fear, sociable love and self-validation. They are quite different in nature, and one can have either one without the other, depending on one's treatment by one's parents or providers.

Sociable love & self-validation: love & fear.

Love is other-directed and in itself disregarding of oneself. Self-validation is self-directed and, taken by itself, based on fear of the moral community and of one's own consciousness. Love of members of the moral community does not motivate self-validation but rather the esteem for the individualities of others. This is not to say that self-validation is selfish, since to be concerned to treat others as being important to oneself in the same way as one is oneself cannot be called selfish.

Moral Teaching:

If the parent indicates disappointment when the child behaves in a way that is contrary to the principle of a moral community, this is a loss of individuality for the child. Consequently, the child learns to fear acting contrary to the principle of a moral community. This is acquiring honour. Honour is a form of self-validation — fear of falling short in treating others as important in the way that one is important to oneself. Teaching a small child is not giving lectures but showing emotions of commendation and disappointment. A young child is keenly sensitive to the emotions of its providers.[27] And it soon learns to interpret the expression of those emotions.

The Family and Larger Communities:

The family is the initial moral community, and in many species as well as for some humans the only one. This may be a nuclear family (as a vixen and her cubs) or an extended family (as a pack of wolves). Human moral communities also began as extended families, but as these coalesced into larger societies those larger societies also became moral communities — by necessity, because that larger society could not function well as an economic community unless it was also a moral community.

Ethics is not one of the optional goods of life, to be cultivated by those who "like that sort of thing". It is the indispensable precondition for even minimal prosperity, for the very existence of a human society. Even brigands

---

[27]See "Some Special Necessary Patterns" on dynamic complementation.

must have a degree of ethics if they are not to destroy their privileges by wars among themselves. This needs to be said in a society that seems to be desperately engaged in the attempt to avoid economic disaster, at both the individual and the societal levels. But how ironic that this should be so in the very society that has finally succeeded in making it possible for everyone to live in economic prosperity and enjoy the pleasures of a life freed from perpetual toil! What have we done to miss that opportunity? The answer is that we have overlooked the indispensability of ethics; we have not noticed that every notch upwards in the quality of life is made possible by a corresponding notch upwards in the quality of moral attitudes, and every notch by which we allow moral attitudes to slip downward deprives us of a notch in the quality of life.

Five Grades of Moral Participation:
We can distinguish five grades of participation in a moral community:

1. Love combined with honour.

2. Love without honour.

3. Honour without love (truthful self-validation).

4. Self-validation by appearances (compromised as to truthfulness).

5. Amorality.

These are not five personality types, although there are persons fitting each of these types. But most of us are sometimes in one grade and sometimes in another, and usually in a mixture of them.

The four grades below the first are the progressively degenerate forms of moral degeneracy.

The First Form of Moral Degeneracy (Love Without Honour):
Honour is the best form of self-validation. To the degree that one has love, one's self-validation will have the intention of honour, but honour entails thoughtfulness about the effects of one's actions, and one may be negligent of that. Such a person will be negligent of themselves as well as of others. In terms of the properties of the parental instinct, this is to have gratitude and generosity but to lack carefulness and dependability. Morally, it is love without honour; emotionally, it is sociable love without social fear. To such a person others are important in the same way as they are important to themselves, namely in a careless sort of way. But gratitude and generosity

without carefulness and dependability may be ineffective in their good intention, and the same for love without honour. As a parent such a person will probably neglect moral teaching and has probably not received it as a child.

The Second Form of Moral Degeneracy (Honour Without Love):

Some parents are occupied with other interests, such as business or public life, and these interests demand their time, so that they give little affective attention to their children. However, they may be morally responsible and careful to teach their children honour. The effect on the children is that others are not important to them in the impulsive way in which they are important to themselves, but their importance to themselves includes being pleased when they **treat** others as having the same kind of importance that they have for themselves and distressed when they do not. The defect of honour without love is that the conception of what it is to treat the individualities of others as important may be distorted. It may be limited to material needs, conveniences, and luxuries, and elements drawn from social convention to the neglect of the need for love and its expressions. Or it may be limited to notions of propriety, as with the knights of former times, whose sense of honour led them into defending either their own reputation or the reputation of another by mortal combat. Thus, it does not dependably serve the individualities of members of the moral community.

Honour completely devoid of love is probably not possible. If parents had no love and affection at all for their child, either they would be half-hearted in teaching honour, or their apparent indifference to the child other than as something to be shaped would make the child resistant to their teaching. It is abundantly apparent in schools that the really effective teachers are those whose love for students elicits love in return and a spontaneous desire to be creditable in the eyes of the teacher as an expression of love and esteem.

The Third Form of Moral Degeneracy (Self-Validation by Appearances):

Self-validation may take two forms: seeking to **actually be** a creditable member of the moral community (which is honour), or seeking to **be perceived** as a creditable member of the moral community, by oneself and by others. When one feels one's creditability to suffer a loss or to be threatened, one's first impulse is to restore the **perception** of one's creditability. Thus, when we feel slighted in conversation, we impulsively defend ourselves, as often as not violating the truth in doing so. When that state of alarm subsides and deliberation is possible, we may react to the longer-term issue of self-validation in either of the two ways: truthful or untruthful, or a mixture of the two.

A willingness to resort to untruthful self-validation may be due to the influence of parents who have that willingness, whereas children whose parents diligently teach them the importance of honour are likely to be motivated by honour. One's parents are one's primary patterns for shaping one's personality and character, and if they do not appear to find it wrong to compromise truth in the interest of self-validation, one will not feel it to be so wrong as to be prohibited. After all, one must treat oneself as important as well as others.

In the third state of degeneracy one has a moral conscience and is distressed if one thinks one has failed to treat others as important in the same way as oneself. It is just that one is not averse to thinking what is not altogether true, maybe even what is altogether false, in order to avoid thinking ill of oneself. The short route to self-service takes precedence over honour at the moment of action, and then one tries to convince oneself and others that one has really acted honourably. But when honour would not compromise self-service, one will prefer to act honourably.

What does one prefer: the vivacity of others or one's own advantage? This is the underlying distinction that divides the first three grades of moral participation from the fourth and fifth.

The Fourth Form of Moral Degeneracy (The Amoral Person):
This is the child who is provided with the material needs of life but is given neither affectionate demonstrations of its importance to the parents nor teaching of how to deal with a moral community. This child has no means of acquiring a concept of a moral community except in the limited sense of entitlement to being provided with material needs. Having been cared for as to survival needs, they feel that someone ought to provide for them, but without any conception of reciprocation. And their conception of how to deal with others is the same in principle as their conception of how to deal with inanimate objects, that is, by manipulation according to the nature of the object. So this is the level of logistics and control, and a feeling as they mature of injustice at being no longer provided for.

The amoral person is by necessity self-reliant, because of having no sense of mutual emotional importance between persons. In this respect there is an analogy between the amoral person and the culture of the last 2500 years. Having lost a belief in the anthropomorphic gods, people could no longer rely on dreams for advice but must turn to their own intellectual resources. Consequently, ours has been a clever and inventive culture, because of cultivating these traits. Similarly, the amoral person, given the innate resources, tends to become clever and resourceful, and this, combined with a compulsive sense of the need for control, implies that these persons tend to rise to positions of social importance. But in those positions, even supposing they intend to act for the common interests, their sense of the common interests will be devoid of the substance of ethics and any awareness of the importance of ethics for the integrity of the community. Consequently, their governance will tend to the disintegration of the community.

And then there is a disastrous flaw in the amoral person's competence. This is the sense of entitlement to having their needs provided and the sense of injustice at the cessation of that provision as they become adults. This, together with a manipulative approach to dealing with others, makes the amoral person highly sensitive to any failure of others to cooperate with their endeavours. As long as their endeavours are successful, they may have all the appearances of responsible and congenial persons, except for a disturbing lack of sensitivity to the feelings of others. But when setbacks occur, they tend to see those who could be seen as the cause of those setbacks as their enemies. This is likely to affect domestic relations especially, since there they have a good deal of real control. Many cases of battered or murdered wives are undoubtedly the result of this paranoid response. This flaw, of course, may ultimately lead to their downfall.

Because of this flaw, amoral persons less endowed with innate capabilities may develop a hatred of the community that effectively disables them from any constructive participation.

The Good:

How would we find out what the good is? First we must distinguish between the intrinsic good and the effectual good. The problem is to determine what the intrinsic good is, since the effectual good is what is conducive to the intrinsic good.

"Good" has a favourable connotation (except in its cynical uses, which are derived from the primary one). Without that favourable connotation the word is semantically empty. That favourable connotation is reflected in our emotions. We have favourable emotions (approval, liking, desiring) towards what we call "good" in the primary sense of the word.

Favourable emotions are elicited by gains of individuality (positive vivacity), and these are called good. To ask whether these are really good as distinct from apparently good is to ask whether the gains of individuality are real or illusory. And the answer is that favourable emotions can only be elicited by real gains of individuality. These may lead to greater losses of individuality and thus be **effectually** bad. But favourable emotions cannot be false indicators of the **intrinsic** good, because emotion is a response to actual gains or losses of individuality, either of a primary sort or due to comparisons of oneself with others.

Therefore, **gains of individuality (positive vivacity) are intrinsically good.**

But simply to say that positive vivacity is the intrinsic good is not quite accurate. If the intrinsic good is that to which we have favourable emotions (because of itself, not because of something else), then the existence of those favourable emotions is inherent in the goodness of the intrinsic good. Thus, **the intrinsic good is positive vivacity to which someone has favourable emotion.**

This implies that the intrinsic good presupposes consciousness of it. And this is inherent in our initial statement of the meaning of "intrinsically good". Intuitively, if there were no consciousness in the universe, neither would there be good or bad. Whether a star remote from any life explodes (thus having a loss of individuality) or not does not matter. But whether someone suffers distress or not does matter.

The Good & Pleasure:

To be pleased is to be conscious of positive vivacity. If another person has the kind of importance to one that one has for oneself, consciousness of positive vivacity in that person will be positive vivacity in one's own consciousness. In this way one can be pleased by the positive vivacity of another.

The argument just developed shows that pleasure, in the sense of ways of being pleased, is the intrinsic good. But in common usage, "pleasure" usually connotes ways of escaping from responsibilities, some of which one may be pleased with and some of which may not please one at all when indulged. Therefore, the thesis that the intrinsic good is pleasure has always been contested. However, if we say "enjoyment" rather than "pleasure", the thesis seems more plausible, since "enjoyment" does not carry the connotation of escaping from responsibility. One can enjoy fulfilling one's responsibilities.

What one is pleased with depends on the level of one's moral participation and on the temporal scope of one's consciousness. If one thinks of long-term consequences and prospects, one will be pleased or displeased by things that would be objects of indifference to someone with a very short-term outlook. Then, since what one is pleased with is positive vivacity, the greater the positive vivacity, the more one is pleased. And the greater

The intrinsic good: enjoyment of enhanced living.

the individuality (integrity of the whole person and vitality), the greater the potential vivacity. Therefore, **the longer is the reach of one's outlook into future and past, the greater is the potentiality of being pleased.**

And since what one is pleased with is positive vivacity, we can suggest as a name for the intrinsic good, **"the enjoyment of enhanced living".**

Good and Bad Are Opposites:

Intrinsic good is positive vivacity; intrinsic bad is negative vivacity. These are opposite in kind, not merely higher and lower on the same scale.

Effectual good is conduciveness to positive vivacity; effectual bad is conduciveness to negative vivacity. These also are opposite in kind, not merely higher and lower on the same scale.

Sociable Love & Desiring the Good of Others:

Sociable love is desire for and pleasure in the presence of members of one's community in a state of high vivacity. Then, since one's intrinsic good is positive vivacity of which one is conscious, sociable love is desiring the intrinsic good of others.

A Good Person:

A good person is one who is **effectually** good. This is a person who has both sociable love and honour — a good heart and a true heart. One's good is in contrast to one's goodness. One's good is what is conducive to one's own high vivacity. One's goodness is one's intentional conduciveness to high vivacity in others.

In the monotheistic religions there is a tradition of a dichotomy of **essentially** good persons and essentially not good persons. This tradition accurately reflects the difference between the attitude of sociable love and honour (gratitude, generosity, carefulness, and dependability) and other general moral attitudes. I say an **attitude** of sociable love and honour

Desire for the vivacity of others.

to take account of those who may be deficient in spontaneous love and honour but have enough of them to appreciate their importance. Such a person may have an attitude of accepting self-validation by appearances when moral compromises can serve their economic interests in a major way and may even on occasion think an amoral attitude is appropriate. And such a person may become convinced that all such deviations from love and honour are both unjustifiable and contrary to their interests and therefore adopt that attitude. This is being converted to the traditional religious conception of an essentially good person (the "saved", the "righteous").

Moral perfection is a practical impossibility, since no one is exempt from forgetfulness and blunders. But the quality of life of a society (the degree to which it is essentially safe and pleasant or unsafe and nasty) is determined by the comparative prevalence of this state of character — gratitude, generosity, carefulness, and dependability — the qualities that are needed in order to effectively treat others as important in the way that one is important to oneself. So religious tradition is essentially right in thinking there is this dichotomy between the good and the less than good.

Sociable love Is Directly Conducive to One's Own Good:
An animal with the parental instinct has greater vivacity than one without it (other things being equal).

☐ An animal with the parental instinct has images of contributing to the vivacity of the young and of seeing them in states of high vivacity, images inherent either in desire or in its gratification.

☐ These states of consciousness have the vivacity of the images.

☐ Only animals with the parental instinct have such states of consciousness. Therefore, they have greater vivacity than animals without it.

The same argument applies to those who have sociable love in comparison with those who lack it. Therefore, sociable love is directly conducive to one's own intrinsic good, which is vivacity of which one is conscious — enjoyment of enhanced living.

The Scope of Sociable Love & One's Enjoyment:
The wider the scope of one's sociable love the greater the opportunity for being conscious of a high state of vivacity in others, either actual or as desired. Therefore, the

Sociable love is enjoyable.

wider the scope of one's sociable love the greater is one's potential enjoyment.

Universal Sociable Love:
To have sociable love for living things in general is to maximize one's potential enjoyment of the vivacity of others. But what are the implications for individuals of species remote from our own and perhaps our enemies, as objects of sociable love?

☐ First, the primary object of sociable love is not the material presence of others but their **vivacity**. And to desire their vivacity is to desire their **individualities**.

☐ The individuality as a whole of an individual is primarily due to its external relationships

☐ These include ecological relationships.

- ☐ Therefore, sociable love for individuals of an alien species includes desire for ecological relationships that maximize the individualities and the vivacity of individuals of that species.

- ☐ One may desire relationships that would maximize the individualities and vivacity of individuals of a species without knowing what such relationships would be.

- ☐ It follows that to have universal sociable love one need not have any particular ecological model in mind as that which one desires. It also follows that universal sociable love does not preclude raising animals and slaughtering them for food. But it would lead us to be concerned with treating them, not merely humanely, but so as to maximize their enjoyment of enhanced living. What may go unnoticed by some is that herds of domestic animals for food would not exist if they were not destined for slaughter, so the question of how they are treated presupposes that they will be slaughtered.

- ☐ We must attack our enemies, such as cockroaches, if we are to respect our own individualities. But an attitude of sociable love will affect the manner in which we do so and in general how we control their populations.

This is an issue of attitudes. As I have said, given the best attitudes, policies consistent with them will likely evolve.

Happiness:
Happiness is enjoyable, but happiness is not the same as enjoyment. Etymologically, it connotes chance and luck and means much the same as "good luck", as in "hapless". The emotion of happiness is a feeling of being in general well used by the world and by other persons. As such, it is a form of gratitude — a feeling of being benefited and an inclination to respond with generosity.

Happiness = gratitude.

Gratitude is an attitude as well as an emotion.[28] It is a willingness to perceive one's good or ill fortune on the basis of points of good fortune rather than points of ill fortune, to see how the world is using one in terms of how it is using one well rather than in terms of how it is mistreating one. Thus, one tends to be grateful for benefits rather than resentful of mistreatment. An attitude of gratefulness for benefits is the key to happiness. Of course, the more predominant one's benefits are the happier one can be. But without the attitude one will not be happy, regardless of benefits and

---

[28]See "Attitudes" in "Consciousness, Choice, & Reasoning".

harms. If one estimates how the world treats one by how much it mistreats one, one will always find something to resent. The most fortunate person in the world will be unhappy with such an attitude, and examples are not hard to find.

These attitudes are like an electronic valve or amplifier: a complaining attitude shuts off the enjoyment of enhanced living, and a grateful attitude amplifies it. Moreover, a complaining attitude creates displeasure all by itself, since one can always imagine that things might have been better than they were. And a grateful attitude diminishes the displeasure of negative vivacity by reducing attention to it.

Happiness & Sociable Love:

Gratitude carries with it a tendency to respond in kind — with generosity in response to well treatment. Thus, a happy attitude is conducive to an attitude of sociable love.

Grades of Moral Participation & Degrees of Enjoyment:

The amoral person is in an almost perpetual state of alarm because of the constant need to maintain or improve control. This person has the lowest degree of enjoyment. The person willing to seek self-validation by appearances rather than reality is also always subject to a state of alarm, since others may become aware of the compromises with truth that have been used to maintain creditability. Probably they are aware of them, but they may become intolerant of them. This person therefore has the second lowest degree of enjoyment.

Comparing the person with both love and honour with the person with love but not honour, the latter's good heartedness is often ineffectual in its good intentions, with the result that one's good intentions are frustrated and creditability with others suffers. Consequently, the former's enjoyment is greater. Then, the person with honour but not love has the benefit of creditability on the basis of honour but not the creditability in the form of reciprocal love that is normally given to the person with love and honour. The persons with love but not honour and with honour but not love are perhaps on a par as to enjoyment.

In short, the person with love and honour (gratitude, generosity, carefulness, and dependability) has tranquillity that the others lack, and the greater the departure from love and honour the greater the loss of tranquillity.

Right and Wrong:

"Bad" is the contrary of "good", intrinsic or effectual. "Wrong" means **intentionally antagonistic** to the good, intrinsic or effectual. "**Ethically** wrong" means intentionally antagonistic to the good of other members of one's moral community, or to what is conducive to it.

Actions that have bad effects on other members of one's moral community may do so accidentally. This does not make them antagonistic to the good of those others. To be antagonistic to the good of other members of one's moral community is to be intentionally conducive to bad effects.

The intrinsic good is positive vivacity of which someone is conscious — the enjoyment of enhanced living. Therefore, what is wrong is what is intentionally antagonistic to the enjoyment of enhanced living, or to what is conducive to the enjoyment of enhanced living.

"Right" has two meanings, ethically obligatory (that is, it would be wrong to intend otherwise), and ethically permissible (that is, not wrong).

Right & Wrong Are Opposites:

What is wrong is intentionally against the good. What is right (in either sense) is not intentionally against the good. As with good and bad, these are opposites, not merely higher and lower on the same scale.

Duty:

To accept membership in a moral community is to undertake to regard other members as important in the same way as one is important to oneself and to assume that one is important to them in the same way as they are important to themselves. Other members have made the same undertaking, so that one has undertaken to be dependable as well as to depend on others. To violate one's undertaking to be depended on and to be dependable is to act as if one had revoked one's membership in the moral community — without in fact revoking it. It is to invite other members to view one as no longer a member.

But how voluntary is that undertaking? In the case of an artificial community such as a club, membership is not imposed, though of course others may try to persuade one to join. But in the case of a natural community, if the dynamics of parental love are in order, one is drawn into the community by the spontaneous tendency to reciprocate that love. And this continues as one is introduced to and welcomed into larger communities. In other words, others become important to one, not by one's choice but by the dynamics of the moral community. And one's undertaking to regard those others as important in the same way as one is important to oneself and to assume that one is important to them in the same way as they are important to themselves is inherent in that process.

Thus, one's undertaking grows as other persons become important to one and is then generalized. Thus, doing one's duty is not primarily being true to one's acceptance of membership.

It is being true to the importance of other members.

But why cannot one arbitrarily decide to exclude particular individuals from one's moral community and so be relieved of duty towards them?

□ Under what conditions would one be considering those options?

□ The beings one was thinking of excluding from one's moral community must have seemed to be candidates for inclusion.

□ In that case, one must have attached some importance to them of the same kind that one had for oneself, either by feeling some love for them or by feeling some compunction that one ought to give them the kind of importance one had for oneself.

To do one's duty is to be true to others.

□ In either case, they have satisfied the conditions for membership in one's moral community, and one has a duty to treat them as such. So the issue is not decidable arbitrarily.

Thus, this account of ethics is not a social contract theory, except for artificial moral communities such as clubs or circles of cronies. One can choose whether to belong to such a community or not, and if one chooses to one is bound by the understanding that defines it. But a natural moral community is defined naturally. One finds oneself in relationships in which others have some importance to one of the same kind as one's importance to oneself. Or one enters relationships on such terms.

Not a social contract

Or one enters relationships on other terms and they develop in that way, just because the parties to them are social animals with the early experience of social animals. The exception to this is the case of the pure amoral person, who has been deprived of that experience except for being provided with sustenance and thereby feeling entitled to it.

Does the amoral person have moral duties? If a person is incapable of attaching importance to others of the same kind as one has for oneself, how can they be bound by moral duties? The amoral person is incapable of being moved by moral duties as such, since the amoral person has no such concept. But from the point of view of others, the amoral person is a member of the moral community in the same way as all the others. Therefore, they are justified in attributing moral duties to the amoral person and applying the same sanctions as in other cases.

Is God a Member of Our Moral Community?

To be a member is either (a) to have membership conferred on one, or (b) to participate as a member, which is equivalent to undertaking to be a member.

To participate as a member is to have moral attitudes and conduct toward other members.

God has the equivalent of moral attitudes (not by volition but by necessity) in the transcendent relationships.

God is like a member.

God has the equivalent of moral conduct in creating us, in giving us moral conscience through the transcendent relationships Creation, Truth, and Beneficence, and soul and spirit through Rootedness and Influence. And this is conferring membership in a moral community on us, a community that includes God.

Therefore, God fulfills the equivalent of (b), and this suffices to establish that God is equivalent to a member of our moral community.

God confers membership on us.

Therefore, we have a duty to act as members in relation to God.

To act as a member in relation to God is to cultivate attitudes and conduct in accordance with the transcendent relationships. This amounts to cultivating sociable love and honour. Therefore, this is our duty.

Our duty: to treat God as a member.

Is God a Person After All, Then?

Based on conclusions drawn so far, the following are some personal characteristics that God **does not have**:

- [ ] God is not the ruler of the universe. On the contrary, God is governed by nature, that is, by the existing patterns and especially the necessary patterns. God acts independently of nature only in the creation of particles, one at a time, and then biased by nature.
- [ ] God is not the designer of the universe, or to have a plan for its future. The nearest God comes to this is to be conscious of tendencies, both long-term and short-term. But the tendencies are dictated by nature, not the initiatives of God.
- [ ] God does not have transcendent volitions. Transcendent volitions would have structure, but the creative factor is outside the category of structure. God's volitions are in the creation of particles.

☐ God does not have volitions with respect to events on a human scale. As the "will of the universe" the creative factor acts as a will only in the creation of particles as biased by the tendencies given by nature.

☐ God is not able to converse with us in a way that is equivalent to the way we can converse with each other. God is the agent of nature and is related to us through the transcendent relationships. We can talk to God if we wish, but God replies only by continuing to present us with the patterns of the transcendent relationships. Like the dead, God speaks to us by setting an example.

God **does** have the following characteristics that may be considered personal:

☐ God acts by volition in creating particles, freely selecting which potentiality to actualize.

☐ God is conscious of both short- and long-term tendencies and in that way may be said to foresee the future, not the actual future, which has no existence prior to occurring, but probable futures.

☐ God experiences pleasure and distress at the gains and losses of individuality of individual processes.

☐ God is a member of our moral communities.

   ▪ God has the equivalent of moral attitudes in Creation, Truth, and Beneficence.

   ▪ God communicates through our conscience by setting an ideal moral example in Creation, Truth, and Beneficence.

   ▪ God has the equivalent of moral conduct in creating us and giving us individuality through Beneficence.

Does God have mind, soul, and spirit?

Mind: Let us say that an entity has a mind if it has emotions, images, volitions, points of view, and self-concepts.

❑ We have seen that God has emotions.

❑ The universe itself and distinctive portions of it may be said to be God's images.

❑ The creation of a particle is an act of volition.

❑ The transcendent relationships qualify as God's self-concepts, since they are relationships between the creative factor and objects that define God.

❑ God does not have points of view, however. Points of view belong to individual processes, in which the creative factor is not God but the will of that process. **However, this, I think, does not imply that God does not have a mind. Rather, it implies that God's mind is always cosmic in scope and never local.**

Soul: One's soul is one's deep nature. In the case of a human this is the reason for identifying soul with rootedness in patterns. In the case of God this applies to Beneficence. But Creation and Truth are themselves aspects of God's deep nature. Thus, God may be said to have a soul.

Spirit: God's influence as a set of patterns is the divine spirit, the foundation for everything in human life that is founded on the parental instinct and love.

Therefore, if to have mind, soul, and spirit is to be a person, God is a person.

An important question for many people is whether God responds to our prayers. "Prayer" can be requests for one's own benefit or for the benefit of others. Or it can be seeking communion with God.

Taking it in the latter sense, contemplating Creation, Truth, and Beneficence may lead one to a consciousness of these as real concrete relationships. And it is likely to make one more sensitive to their importance as patterns and more inclined to have attitudes analogous to those patterns. Contemplating Rootedness and Influence is likely to make one define oneself and habitually think of oneself in terms of soul and spirit as well as in terms of a process in temporal space. God "speaks to us" by example, not by conversing, and to listen to God is to pay attention to God's example.

God's example is of two kinds: the transcendent relationships, and God's action in creating particles. The lesson of the latter pattern according to the present account is that events on a human scale are not objects of creative action but objects of tendency. The creation of particles is also the partial creation of larger-scale events, so that tendencies on a human scale affect events on a human scale through affecting the creation of particles. God does not control them; we do so only indirectly. This makes God in one way less of a person. But in another way it makes God more of a person, in that it relieves God of responsibility for catastrophes and of the evil deeds of humans — the latter are the responsibility of those persons, not attributable to God.

But can we influence God by our prayers? This has to be a matter of having an effect on tendencies. If one can form a concept of a desirable outcome that is in close similarity to the person or persons one wishes that outcome to happen to, this may be a special pattern that will strengthen the tendency for that outcome to come about. If the outcome is a genuine good, one could say one has gained God's favour, but it is just as appropriate to say that one has manipulated nature. If the outcome is not a genuine good, one has only manipulated nature and practised sorcery. The reason for this is that "gaining God's favour" would mean bringing Beneficence into play, and that only applies to good potentialities.

Setting a Good Example:

Other persons are patterns for our moral attitudes and conduct, and we are patterns for the attitudes and conduct of others. And, as I said earlier, we are patterns for potential lives throughout the universe and for all time to come. As **ethical** patterns for potential lives, to the degree that we are patterns of love and honour, we are analogous to God (to Beneficence and Truth). This would make us special patterns combining with these highly prevalent patterns so as to give potentialities of love and honour high potency. Added to this is the general pattern of ethics, which is universal to species of social animals, whereas other characteristics such as skill and competence depend on factors more peculiar to the species. From the conclusion of the preceding section we can infer that it is our duty to set as good an **ethical** example as we can. Our example with respect to skill and competence has far less potential efficacy.

However, duty is not a motive and does not of itself induce us to do it. What incentive is there, therefore, for doing one's duty? Any failure to do our duty will be a loss of individuality, since our individuality is greatly enhanced by the closeness of the analogy with God. If we are **conscious** of our analogy with God as ethical patterns, that loss of individuality will be much greater. Thus, we have reason to fear the consequence of failing in our duty. On the other side, when we are conscious of succeeding in doing our duty, we experience a gain of individuality, so that, although the duty itself is sometimes unpleasant or even agonizing, success in doing it is pleasant.

So the reward of setting a good example is positive vivacity, and the punishment for failing to do so is shame or remorse.

Setting an Example for All Time:

Let us pull some of these threads together.

Our example shapes future souls.

□ Our responsibility is primarily to children and young people.[29] Ethical examples are more efficacious than non-ethical examples. They are also more efficacious across species of social animals than non-ethical examples are, because

---

[29]See "Responsibility".

social animals of all species are alike in the prolonged and intimate care of the young.[30]

☐ Setting an example for all time is setting an example for the potential children and young people and the potential young of all social species of all future time.

☐ Patterns set by individual lives shape the souls of later lives.[31]

☐ The widest scope of one's sociable love brings the greatest vivacity.[32]

☐ It is our duty to cultivate attitudes and conduct in accordance with the transcendent relationships.[33]

Setting a good example for all time.

☐ Success in doing our duty is pleasant, and failing in our duty is alarming, a loss of the individuality of self-validation.[34]

☐ Also on the theme of self-validation, it is urgent for each of us to be important to those who are important to us, namely other members of our moral community. To set a good example for all time is to be important in a favourable sense to other members. To set a bad example for all time is to be important in an unfavourable sense.

☐ God is a member of our moral community. If we are conscious of the transcendent relationships and their importance, to be important to God in a favourable or unfavourable sense will be especially important for our self-validation.

☐ Therefore, we have a great deal to gain or lose by setting the best ethical example we can or neglecting to do so with the consciousness that it is a potentially effective pattern for all future time.

Moral Attitudes & Moral Emotions:

Sociable love is an emotion, but one can have an attitude of cultivating sociable love.[35] One thinks of other members of one's moral community, however one defines that community, as having individuality, and one thinks of their individualities as sacred,[36] as being of pre-eminent importance and not to be tampered with, just as good parents think of their children.

---

[30]See Preceding section.

[31]See "Psychosomatic Effects" in "Individuality".

[32]"The Scope of Sociable love & One's Enjoyment".

[33]"But is God a Member of Our Moral Community?"

[34]"Duty".

[35]See "Attitudes" in "Consciousness, Choice, & Reasoning".

[36]See "But is There a God, Then?" in "Transcendence".

However, love is also desire for and pleasure in the presence of the other's individuality. And the attitude of sociable love is one of intending to take delight in the individualities of other members of the community, and, broadly speaking, in their presence (their particular individualities may not be such as to inspire delight, but as individualities they are, and one thinks of that). But what is presence? There are degrees of presence, from the intimate embrace of one who is closest to us to the mere awareness of the existence of those whom we regard as members of our community but whom we would rather keep at a distance.

Recall the three classes of emotion based on three necessary patterns.[37] Two of these are evoked by variations in one's own individuality or prospects for individuality, and the third is evoked by comparing one's own potentialities (capabilities, wealth, opportunities) with those of another or others. Broadly speaking, the emotions of variations of individuality are healthy emotions, while those of comparing oneself with others may or may not be. The reason is that the emotions of variations of individuality always tell one the truth about one's immediate intrinsic good, whereas the emotions of

Emotions of comparison express moral attitude.

comparing oneself with others usually do not. Such comparisons express one's moral attitude at the moment. They may express a willingness to justify a degraded moral attitude (as in the case of envy or smugness) or a desire to improve one's moral attitude (as in being inspired by a "role model"), or a desire to have an ideal moral attitude. These attitudes are expressed in one's choice of standards with which to compare oneself and one's use of that comparison — whether that standard is taken to be one to be followed (if one can) or one to be avoided.

If one desires to emulate an ideal moral standard, one will compare oneself with what one takes to be an ideal moral standard. The objectively ideal moral standard is the combination of the transcendent relationships Creation, Truth, and

And affect moral attitude.

Beneficence with the idealized parental instinct (gratitude, generosity, carefulness, and dependability).

---

[37]See "Necessary Patterns for These Emotions" in "Consciousness, Choice, & Reasoning".

Because of the imperative of self-validation, comparisons of oneself with others are automatic, and one cannot altogether avoid the consequent emotions — feelings of inferiority or superiority. But one can avoid the secondary emotions due to the conceptual use one makes of the comparisons, such as envy or contempt. The former are due to one's need for a place of security and importance in one's moral community. The latter are due to specifically **ethical** attitudes. Whether or not one has contempt for those whose place in the community is inferior to one's own depends on whether one conceives the individualities of others to be sacred or not. Whether or not one feels envy for those whose place in the community is superior to one's own depends on whether one conceives one's own individuality to be sacred or not. These are fundamental ethical attitudes and are better or worse in absolute terms. **Which of them a particular person has is not to be regarded as a sacred feature of that person's individuality.** Ethical attitudes are not idiosyncrasies on a par as to individuality; rather they are determinants of the degree of one's individuality — to have worse ethical attitudes is to have a lower degree of wholeness and distinctiveness. A poor ethical attitude should not inspire respect but loathing and pity, as being harmful to others and a deprivation of enjoyment for themselves.

Comparisons of oneself with others are not to be confused with the fact that every person is a pattern that may significantly influence others, especially if they are conscious of that pattern. The principle here is causality by patterns.

Stabilities & Instabilities of Self-Validation:

Our social need is to be seen as a creditable member of the moral community. When someone behaves as if we were deficient in creditability, we may respond in terms of either of the two types of emotion — those of gains and losses of individuality or prospects for individuality, or those of comparing ourselves with others. We may interpret their behaviour either (1) as a judgment that we have failed in sociable love or honour, or (2) as a comparison of our creditability with theirs. (1) We may feel a loss of creditability and a need to improve in sociable love and/or honour — this is the response of shame. Or (2) we may suppose that they are accusing us of being less creditable than they are. And we may respond to this

Positive feedback in self-validation

comparison by accusing them of being less creditable than ourselves. If they then respond in the same way, a pattern of reciprocal recrimination is set up. This is a degenerative process with progressive losses of self-validation on both sides. Entering on this response (2) introduces an instability into the dynamics of self-validation.

On the other hand, the response of shame (1) confers creditability on the other person. This is a confirmation of their membership in the moral community. As such it is a gain of individuality, and a gain of individuality carries a tendency to seize that opportunity to seek a still greater gain. In other words, they are encouraged to be even more creditable than they are, thus gaining the reward of greater moral esteem. Also, shame is itself creditable and tends to elicit a conferral of creditability on oneself, which has the same effect on oneself as it has on the other. This (1), therefore, is a stabilizing response, encouraging all parties to live up to their membership in the moral community.

Pride & Shame:

Pride and shame respectively are gains or losses of individuality in the consciousness of one's participation in a community. This defines **true** pride or shame. Pride has been called the worst of the "deadly sins". This refers to **false** pride, which is a gain of individuality in the consciousness of **oneself** as a participant in a community — false because the cause of a gain of individuality is not oneself as such but one's participation in the community. Humility, the contrary of false pride, is the attribution of whatever is creditable in oneself to the community or particular members of it rather than to oneself. True pride is a gain of individuality in the consciousness, not of **oneself** but of one's **participation** in the community.

Thus, teachers with true pride are proud of their students (as being theirs), and students with true pride are proud of their school and their fellow students (as being theirs). When their students fail in creditability as members of the school community on occasion, teachers with true pride are ashamed of their students **as being students they would normally be proud of**. This elicits true shame in those students.

This distinction is an instance of the distinction between the two kinds of emotion. In false pride or shame one feels superior or inferior

Pride & shame, true & false

to others in one's community. In true pride or shame one feels a gain or loss of individuality in one's participation in a community. The emotions of superiority and inferiority have the effect of setting members of the community against one another; in other words they are in opposition to the principle of a community. The healthy emotions have the effect of encouraging them to support one another.

True pride and true shame are the cornerstones of a healthy moral community and the teachers of undistorted sociable love and honour.

Two False Conceptions of a Community:
1) A community of amoral persons — selfishness without honour: It is understood by those who have this conception (as it is by amoral persons) that one needs the cooperation of others to pursue the maximization of one's individuality — conceived in terms of acquisition and control. One

An amoral community is unworkable.

would gain that cooperation by the following methods, in order of preference: (a) trade advantageous to both; (b) cajolery and flattery; (c) bribery; (d) trickery; (e) coercion. These would be preferred in that order because willing cooperation is preferred to unwilling cooperation.

This conception is false because a community based on that principle could only exist briefly. If there were no functioning parental instinct, there might be babies born, but the care of them would not suffice for their survival in sufficient numbers. This conception of a community is a masculine one; women with few exceptions have enough of the maternal instinct to see it as implausible that there could be a community that took care of infants only with a view to making them useful later on.

(2) A community based on trade — selfishness with honour: The idea here is that benefits received must be reciprocated with equivalent benefits returned. As to how to determine what is equivalent; the principle in the case of competent adults is that this is what is agreeable to both parties. Thus it is considered legitimate to "make a killing" provided both parties agree. Even the care of children has often been conceived as trade, the idea being that the child owes benefits to the parents in return for having been cared for — the duties of children is a common traditional notion. This is not at all the same as the child performing services for the parent out of gratitude. Trade incorporates the principle of equivalence; gratitude and love have no such principle. Deeds of gratitude and love are not measured out like merchandise

A community based on trade is unworkable.

but given without conditions on benefits received previously or in return, because of the importance to oneself of the individuality of the other person, just as deeds for the sake of one's own individuality have no other motive but the importance of one's individuality to oneself. The degree of one's gratitude may depend on the benefits received or expected, but actions out of gratitude are measured out only according to one's resources and what one thinks would benefit the other.

Relationships of trade may be necessary in human communities, but a moral community could not be based on trade. If mothers in particular cared for their infants only conditionally on "being paid" later, the investment would not be attractive.

Nor would trade itself work without an underlying foundation of sociable love. Trade based on pure selfishness would not really be honourable. If the maximization of one's own individuality is the only aim, the opportunistic nature

Trade presupposes sociable love.

of the tendency would lead to seizing opportunities for dishonest dealings, provided one thought the dishonesty could be concealed. And if one's position appeared to be unassailable, one would resort to open coercion. Examples in actual business to illustrate this principle are not unfamiliar.

Reason, Ethics, & Self-Validation:

Taking reason (as distinct from rationalization or simply acting on the impulse of emotions) to entail objectivity, this, as we saw,[38] presupposes a foreground of consciousness representing a point of view detached from oneself and one's interests. That being so, considerations of ethics and self-validation enter into rational reasoning not as affecting the

Reason need not be ethical

person but only as affecting the similarities of options with patterns in consciousness.

It follows that reason can be used in a totally amoral way, just as effectively for the planning of a crime or atrocity as for deliberating on what one ought morally to do. Reason is as available to the amoral person who has turned to evil, as it is to the person rich in sociable love and strong in honour.

On the Consequences of One's Actions:

That one should take the consequences of one's actions into account is obvious. That one should do good and avoid doing harm, both in the immediate effect of one's action and in the remote or peripheral effects, is just as obvious. This statement seems to imply a Benthamite principle of utilitarianism, a calculus of good and bad effects, as the appropriate means of

---

[38]See "Objectivity" in "Consciousness, Choice, & Reasoning".

deciding what one ought to do, or, given the practical impossibility of implementing that principle, some rules of thumb reflecting the major statistical properties of the consequences of common actions in general.

While some such rules of thumb are useful (especially those that advise actions analogous to the transcendent relationships Creation, Truth, and Beneficence), in general weighing the good and bad consequences of actions is of only limited effectiveness — limited to the obvious consequences. And then, how should one weigh the importance of consequences to oneself or to those close to one against consequences to remote persons or other animals? Moreover, the value of such a deliberation is conditional on the steadfastness and consistency of one's intention to do good and avoid doing harm. In other words, it is conditional on one's moral attitude. This leads us to consider moral attitudes and motives.

Kant points out that what is of essential importance is that one should have a good will, and he is eloquent in giving examples to illustrate the meaning of that, namely that others should be important to one in the same way as one is important to oneself (though he does not say it in that way).[39] Competence in exercising one's good will to good effect, while valuable, is not of such value as to carry **any** weight against the importance of a good will. Charles Dickens, too, was well aware of this principle. In *Dombey and Son* for example, Captain Cuttle is a model of someone with a good will. Of competence in implementing it he has none and bungles every attempt to help out the young persons he wishes to help. But in the longer run it is Captain Cuttle who is mainly instrumental in bringing things to a good end.

That, of course, is a novel and cannot count as empirical evidence. But it may draw our attention to relations of cause and effect that are evident to the imagination and reason. Without good ethical attitudes, knowledge of consequences, however adequate, does not carry enough weight against self-interest to be effective. With good ethical attitudes, one will do the sorts of things that are likely to have the best consequences, namely actions that are attentive to and promotive of the individualities of others.

There are two ways in which one's actions have effects. The obvious one is by way of a chain of intermediate connecting events proceeding through temporal space from the cause to the effect. It is these effects that are largely unpredictable in practice. But the other one is through causality by patterns — as a pattern for future potentialities. These effects are predictable (as to the kind of effects if not the degree), namely as being similar to the pattern. And these effects are not only on those who observe the pattern and are influenced by it as a conscious pattern; they are also remote, and just as predictable regardless of how remote they are.

---

[39]In The Foundations of the Metaphysics of Morals and also in The Critique of Practical Reason.

So we come back to the importance of attitudes, and especially moral attitudes.

13 CULTURE

What Is a Culture?

I would define a culture as a shared and cultivated set of attitudes. Such a set of attitudes is expressed in such things as architecture, landscape, and the arts, as well as customs and social conventions of propriety and manners. These expressions are also the means of cultivating the attitudes that constitute the essence of the culture.

Two Levels of Culture:

There are distinctive cultures expressed in social conventions of propriety, manners, styles of clothing, architecture, and the like; and there is universal culture consisting of ethics. I say universal, because every viable community acknowledges and teaches in some form the fundamental principle of ethics, that others are to be important to one in the same way as one is important to oneself, that being the basis of the community's viability.

Universal culture is ethics.

The indispensability of ethics to the viability of a culture implies that culture is peculiar to the social animals. All the things associated with culture — all interests and pleasures over and above those immediately pertaining to survival (of the individual and the species) presuppose ethics and belong only to the social animals; similarly for degradations such as intentional malice, cruelty, crime and war.

What Is a Good Culture?

The intrinsic good applies only to living individuals (which are capable of high levels of vivacity). Therefore, a good culture is conducive to the intrinsic good — effectually good. But to whose intrinsic good?

It must be primarily the participants in the culture, for the following reasons:

❑ Everyone's basic tendency is to take the potentiality that offers the greatest immediate vivacity as a total tendency (tendency in the universe + tendency due to consciousness), in other words to follow the steepest gradient of their own potential individuality (conscious + unconscious).

Goodness begins at home.

❑ One's own individuality has potentially steeper apparent gradients than the individualities of others, exceptions being rare outside one's immediate family.

❑ Members of one's family are participants in one's culture.

❑ Therefore, for a culture not to give priority to the intrinsic good of its own participants would not be workable — nature would overcome culture.

Therefore, a good culture is, first of all, conducive to the intrinsic good of its own participants.

Cultural Consistency:

To be most effective, a culture must not cultivate conflicting attitudes. What, in particular, does cultural consistency require?

❑ To be conducive to the intrinsic good of its own participants a culture must cultivate ethical attitudes, and the best cultures will cultivate the highest levels of sociable love and honour.

❑ Therefore, consistency requires that the conventional aspects of the culture not oppose the cultivation of sociable love and honour.

    o For example, popular entertainments that celebrate cruelty and violence work against the cultivation of ethical attitudes and harm the culture.

❑ Beliefs and opinions must not contradict the principles of ethics.

    o For example, the widespread view that good and evil (conduciveness to and against the intrinsic good) are not diametrical contraries but complementaries analogous to light and dark tends to undermine the cultivation of sociable love and honour by obscuring their distinction from contempt for the individualities of others and for truth.

❑ Beliefs and opinions must not deny the distinction between ethical culture and conventional culture.

    o For example, the view that ethical norms are "culture-bound" and vary from one culture to another may, as a point of fact, be a partial truth, but it is a falsehood in its suggestion that views about ethics are right or wrong according to their prevalence in the particular culture. Ethical norms need to be distinguished from ethical truths.

Cultures of Obedience & Cultures of Freedom:

In the evolution of human communities, as soon as communities became large enough to require organization and institutions, the functioning of those institutions required that individuals comport themselves consistently with that functioning. Otherwise, the institutions could not function, and members of the community would suffer. This led to a culture in which the principle of obedience to the requirements of the institutions was paramount. Prior to recent times, all organized societies shared this principle. Failure to adhere to it was feared as leading to social chaos and consequent violence and poverty, for it was easily perceived that there was a natural temptation to disobey. Plato, in the **Republic**, takes it for granted that the important question is not what is good for individual persons but what is good for the city-state.

But Plato and Aristotle are beginning to move away from the idea of an obedience culture. They reject the traditional idea that the gods are jealous of their secrets. Aristotle argues, perhaps illogically, that God could not be jealous, because the best thing we can do is to be as godlike as we can, and that entails seeking to understand things as well as we can. The author of the Adam and Eve story thought it obvious that the gods would see it as a trespass on their privileges if humans were to become godlike by eating the fruit of both the tree of knowledge and the tree of life. But Aristotle is thinking of God, not on the model of an emperor or tyrant, jealous of his power and in fear of rivals, but on the model of the ideal father and head of a family, not jealous of his children but eager to set them a good example and give them the best education.

Institution-centred vs. individual-centred culture

In mediaeval Europe, a major move away from obedience culture was made with the courtly love tradition and the idea of a conflict between romantic love and arranged marriage in the interest of family connections. From then until now innumerable romances have been written on the plot of the triumph of marrying for love over marrying for family connections in obedience to family demands.

This draws attention to an interesting fact: Obedience cultures, or those with a literary component, have long contained the seeds of freedom culture in the form of poems and stories about person-to-person interactions and emotions.

In our time, the idea of an individual-centred way of life is being carried around the world by romance novels, Hollywood movies, and soap operas, and in general the symbols of Western culture. When individuals, especially women, get a taste of this idea, they like it.

But even when I was a child obedience culture was still very much alive. Elementary and high school seem in retrospect to have been largely obedience training. It is really since World War II that the individual-centred way of life, with its ideal of personal freedom, has become dominant in Western Europe and North America. (An incidental symptom of this is the decline of the holy orders in the Catholic Church.) The United Nations charter of human rights may have been signed by many nations, but I think, only half-heartedly by most of them. Their deep conviction is that rights belong to the institutions of society and duties belong to individuals. This is why, for example, the Chinese government is deaf to Western criticisms of their "abuses of human rights". Those criticisms seem to them to have no bearing on social reality and the need to avoid disorder. Osama bin Laden and others of his persuasion are, it seems to me, engaged in a rather desperate program of preserving an obedience culture against the onslaught of the popular appeal of American culture. He has said that his program is one of revenge — "You kill us, we kill you," but the deeper motive is that of religious reactionaries everywhere — a rearguard action in defence of obedience culture.

In defence of their view it must be said that freedom culture is more difficult than obedience culture. For freedom culture to be workable, individuals must be educated to a sense of moral responsibility not dependent on the concept of an external authority. In the absence of such an education, the defenders of obedience culture are in the right. And we see what happens in parts of the world where that sort of education is lacking when individuals acquire political power — they see it as an opportunity for wealth and self-aggrandizement. Obedience culture is not to be condemned. Rather, the conditions for the workability of a culture of freedom should be cultivated.

But Is Freedom Culture Inherently Better?

In Western Europe and North America we have come to take it for granted that personal freedom is supremely desirable and a universal right.

But is an individual-centred way of life really better in principle than an institution-centred way of life?

☐ The animal body is the focus of complementation, because it has no rivals for total individuality relative to the volume of temporal space occupied by the body as a process.

☐ Institutions themselves do not act; they do not issue demands on behaviour. Individuals act on behalf of institutions.

☐ In obedience cultures institutions are the beneficiaries of moral conscience. But benefits are to individuals. Without individuals, institutions are both inert and irrelevant.

☐ Serving institutions serves individuals only to the extent that those who act on behalf of the institutions do so with a view to serving individuals.

☐ But in an obedience culture, they will not think in this way. Their sense of ethics is that institutions ought to be important to one in the way that one is important to oneself.

☐ Therefore, obedience culture cannot easily cultivate sociable love and honour according to the real nature of these qualities.

History bears this out. When the ancient kings were, as it was said they ought to be, "the shepherds of their people", thus servants of the people, the people were well served by the state. Even then, these "shepherds" not only cared for their "sheep" but also were attentive to fleecing them. But in many cases they thought only of fleecing them. And the agents of institutions in general to this day are careful to achieve a higher degree of wealth and luxury than is enjoyed by those served by the institutions.

☐ Freedom culture is not necessarily better, but the sense that others ought to be important to one in the way that one is important to oneself is not diverted from individuals to institutions as it is in obedience culture.

☐ Therefore, freedom culture is likely to be better.

From Institutions as Authorities to Institutions as Instruments, from Collective Interests to Common Interests:

In an obedience culture institutions are seen as authorities. In a freedom culture, institutions are seen as instruments of individuals, held in common. This is a shift from a concept of collective interests to a concept of

Institutions have no interests.

common interests, from the interests **of the society** to the interests **of individuals**. In an obedience culture, the interests vested in institutions are seen as collective interests, that is, interests of the community as an entity. In a freedom culture, the interests vested in institutions are seen as common interests, that is, the interests common to many or all of the members of the community. In this respect, freedom culture is congruent with fact, while obedience culture is delusive — institutions themselves have no interests; rather the interests of individuals (either those who act on behalf of the institutions or those served by the institutions) are vested in the institutions. Obedience cultures pretend that institutions have interests; freedom cultures deny this and assert that the interests of those served by the institutions are vested in the institutions and that it is the duty of those who act on behalf of the institutions to adhere to that principle rather than making the institutions instruments of their personal privileges.

Individuals have interests.

Why "Freedom Culture"; Why Not "Individualistic Culture"?

An individual-centred culture frees individuals from subordination to institutions. As such it also deprives individuals of the comfort of being directed by institutions and throws them on the necessity of forming decisions for themselves. But it is not individualistic in the sense of detaching them from the community. The principle of ethics ties them to the community and makes them responsible for other individuals as well as for institutions. Thus, responsibility has been shifted from institutions to individuals. The community has become the responsibility of each individual. This is a great burden, and individuals have a consequent need for something else as a balance to that burden. That "something else" is freedom. It is often said that one needs responsibility to balance freedom. But in the transition from institution-centred culture to individual-centred culture, the individual first acquires responsibility, Freedom is more difficult and is acquired later.

But What Is Freedom?

Freedom is sometimes conceived as absence of constraints and restraints, and sometimes as having a rich variety of options. I will argue that neither of these gets at the essence of freedom.

- ☐ To be cast adrift in outer space (assuming one could live there) would be to be without constraints or restraints, but no one would call this kind of freedom personal freedom. To be free is not only to be free **from** this or that but also to be free **to do** something of value (free to travel, free to attend plays, free to study physics).

- ☐ Therefore, freedom is opportunity.
- ☐ Opportunity precludes prohibitive impediments, but it does not preclude impediments that may be surmounted.

Freedom is opportunity.

- ☐ To **feel** free is to feel heightened vivacity at the contemplation of one's opportunities — to be thrilled at being able to do what one desires to do, what gives one the prospect of high vivacity.
- ☐ Assuming one's opportunities are what one takes them to be, both as to their reality and as to the effect on oneself of realizing them, to feel free is to be free.
- ☐ Therefore, to be free is to have the opportunity of experiencing high levels of vivacity, that is, of achieving one's intrinsic good.
- ☐ The **ideal** of freedom is to have maximum opportunities for maximizing one's vivacity and one's enjoyment of it.

Maximum opportunity to maximize one's vivacity.

- ☐ This implies acting on one's un-coerced volition, but it does not imply acting on one's own initiative *rather than* following the orders of another. If those orders promise maximum opportunities for maximizing one's vivacity, then one will gladly follow them. For example, young children, who lack the knowledge for maximizing their vivacity by their own ingenuity, are eager to follow orders that carry the prospect of freedom.

Opportunity Entails Structure:

Opportunity is opportunity to do something. To do something that realizes high vivacity is to do something that has a structure that realizes potentialities of one's individuality, therefore that continues the development of one's individuality. Such potentialities entail an environment in which such a

A dependable environment

development can occur. For example, to be a musician one must have a teacher and places for practice and for performance. This in turn presupposes the external features of a culture that includes music, with buildings, streets, and so on. This environment must be dependable. Floors must not let one down; walls must not be easily broken through. And the buildings must invite occupancy for their purposes and discourage occupancy for incompatible purposes. In other words, an environment that provides opportunities for one's good also imposes limitations on what one can do or might wish to do. Those limitations are inherent in the opportunities. **To be well defined, the opportunities must also be circumscribed.**

A structured environment

Opportunity must Be Perceptible:

If the person cannot perceive their opportunities, those opportunities are not real. To be perceptible the opportunities must be well defined, and to be well defined they must be circumscribed. The limitations of the environment are necessary for making the opportunities perceptible.

The requirement of perceptibility is especially relevant to young persons and education.

The Environment Is Personal and Social as Well as Structural:

Opportunities are provided by the combination of people and material facilities; and the requirement of structure, dependability and perceptibility applies no less to the people than to the material facilities. Analogous to floors that will not let one down are persons in functional positions who perform those functions reliably. Analogous to walls that cannot be easily broken through are intolerances to certain kinds of behaviour that are reasonably regarded as unacceptable. Analogous to doors that invite entry for taking the opportunities that the building provides but discourage entry for contrary purposes is a welcoming attitude to those who desire the opportunities one is providing and an unwelcoming attitude to those with contrary intentions. Analogous to buildings that invite entry for accepting the opportunities they provide are persons such as teachers and administrators who provide the organization that provides the opportunity for participation.

The qualities of character that these requirements presuppose are those of the parental instinct: gratitude, generosity, carefulness, and dependability.

Do More Options Mean More Freedom?

☐ Suppose one has the opportunity of learning and doing what will most fully maximize one's individuality and vivacity. Then one has no need of any alternative opportunities. To the natural musician, the option of becoming an engineer is irrelevant.

☐ Therefore, not the variety of options but their appropriateness to the capacities and inclinations of members of the community, especially the young, is what is relevant to freedom.

☐ However, the exercise of volition is an essential feature of individuality. Even if one had the opportunity that would most fully maximize one's individuality and vivacity, if one's only alternative to adopting it were to be excluded from participating in the community, one could hardly be said to be free and would not feel free. Therefore, some desirable options are essential to freedom.

☐ Moreover, different individuals have different capacities, and if the community is to provide freedom to all of them, a variety of opportunities sufficient for their various potentialities for individuality and vivacity must be provided.

More options do not mean more freedom.

Therefore, in brief:

1) To be free does not mean to have many options but to have good options.

2) More good options mean freedom for more people.

Civilization:

What is civilization? If we take the urban revolution as a clue to answering this question, the answer that suggests itself is that a civilization is a community that is (1) organized, (2) with a view to providing an abundance of the enjoyment of enhanced living to its members. This is the spirit of the early city-states in contrast with the disciplined culture of the early agricultural societies in

Enjoyment of enhanced living in abundance

which people were thought of as subjugated to the earth goddess. And I think that is what we have in mind when we speak of civilization or refer to a society as civilized.

In any case, the best kind of culture would be one that cultivated the attitude of desiring an abundance of the enjoyment of enhanced living for its participants and willingness to participate in the organization of society in order to achieve that end.

Providing an abundance of the enjoyment of enhanced living to its members may mean providing it to all its members, or it may mean providing it to a privileged minority of its members, or it may mean both — providing it to all members, but more generously to the privileged minority. The first of these meanings gives the word "civilization" its laudatory connotation, and the second gives it its derogatory connotation. The best civilizations historically have perhaps been thought of by their leaders in the first of these ways, but in actual fact they have been of the third type.

For the few or for the many

Organized to what end? The enjoyment of enhanced living is the intrinsic good. I have argued that the most effective way to maximize one's own intrinsic good is to have a maximum of sociable love and honour.[40] It follows that the best culture is one that cultivates an abundance of sociable love and honour. And this form of abundance is the one that leads to other forms, as the natural exercise of sociable love and honour. And of course it follows that the best civilizations will be those that are organized with a view to providing an abundance of the enjoyment of enhanced living to all its members, and to all living things as well, insofar as that is feasible.

Abundance of sociable love

Civilization & Civility: To have an attitude of sociable love and honour is to feel and to think that individualities are sacred .[41] This affects one's manner in interacting with others — the expression of one's emotions and attitudes. One's expressions towards others will express the attitude that their individualities are sacred. This, I think, is what is meant by "civility". Even when it is insincere, it expresses the acknowledgement that one ought to regard the individualities of others as sacred.

Education on the principle of freedom

Civilization & Freedom: A society organized to provide an abundance of the enjoyment of enhanced living for all its members will aim at maximizing

---

[40]See "Sociable Love & One's Own Enjoyment" in "Ethics & Self-validation".

[41]See "Moral Attitudes & Moral Emotions" in "Ethics & Self-Validation".

the opportunities for all its members to maximize their individuality. In other words, it will cultivate the ideal of freedom.

Civilization & Education: An attitude of treating the individualities of others as sacred would lead to education based on the principle of freedom, since this is maximizing the opportunities for young persons to maximize their individuality.

Civilization & Fine Art: I would suggest that what we mean by fine art is art that expresses the sacredness of individuality.

☐   In fine art in the pure sense the only aim of the artist is the excellence of the work itself, in other words, the maximization of its wholeness and distinctiveness.

☐   Since art is fiction, this implies that the work of art expresses the principle that individuality is of pre-eminent importance and not to be tampered with, that is, its sacredness.

This is not to decry other forms of art (decorative art, commercial art, art for social occasions, art for the artist's entertainment) but only to distinguish the peculiar character of fine art.

A good civilization cultivates the attitude that individualities are sacred. The most important way of doing that is by example. Another is by instruction. Another is by fine art. A good civilization needs fine art in order to set an absolute standard of the sacredness of individuality. Without fine art the only standards are those set by the best moral attitudes. And they only set a standard of the sacredness of the individualities of concrete persons, whereas fine art abstracts the idea of individuality from concrete patterns. Religious art, which by intention suggests the transcendent relationships, usually suggests the authority of particular institutions. It is fine art that presents the idea of the sacredness of individuality in its purity. To cultivate the attitude that individualities are sacred, therefore, a civilization needs to cultivate the fine arts. And since the fine arts are generally not commercially viable, a good civilization needs to support them in material ways.

Civilization needs fine art.

Civilization & Fictions: Fictions permit the perception of possibilities not presented in concrete life. This is important in a culture designed to provide an abundance of the enjoyment of enhanced living. We

And beautiful fictions.

need to be able to envision a life that is better than the actual, or a variant of it that is just as good.

For this we need fictions that will serve as patterns for variant forms of the intrinsic good. Patterns for the intrinsic good, when thought of as such, are seen as beautiful, and what is seen as beautiful is seen as a pattern for the intrinsic good — for conscious vivacity and the enjoyment of enhanced living. (The beautiful is not itself the intrinsic good but is analogous to the intrinsic good. The beautiful is to the intrinsic good as the ugly is to distress or misery.)

Civilization needs beautiful fictions. To be organized for providing abundance of the enjoyment of enhanced living to its participants, it needs patterns to put before them to keep reminding them of what the enjoyment of enhanced living really is (as distinct from conditions to envy or to make one be envied) and to give them a desire for abundance of the genuine intrinsic good, as distinct from counterfeits of it, such as affluence or control.

Civilization, Leisure, & Quietude: Because of the organized character of a civilization, it needs a thinking populace. If people are to be disposed to think, they must have a certain amount of quietude. And if thinking is to be to good effect, it must be done in an unhurried way, therefore in quietude & leisure. This is because thinking is a conscious process, but that conscious process arises from an unconscious process with the properties that constitute consciousness. The results of thinking need to be re-evaluated repeatedly, and this means carrying them over from one state of consciousness to another ("sleeping on them"). For this to happen so that they are not lost in distractions requires leisure and quietude.

And needs leisure & quietude.

The Importance of Writing: In the play of consciousness, thoughts tend to be lost in the playfulness of consciousness, which is perpetually creating new thoughts. Writing not only constitutes a memory of thoughts but can also be the material form of thoughts with a structure and precision that thoughts "in one's head" are incapable of. Writing is essential to science and philosophy, and a work such as the present could only be developed over a period of years with the help of writing.

Writing holds thoughts still for examination.

Civilization & Humour: Humour is exploring the boundaries of the acceptable, whether of ethics, or of propriety, or of custom or of logic. The humour of Lewis Carroll is funny because it goes outside the boundaries of logic, propriety, and custom while retaining a quality of acceptability. In doing so it helps to define what those boundaries are. In general, it is important on the one hand to appreciate the principles of the boundaries, which in the cases of ethics and logic are constant and exact, and on the other hand to appreciate the inexactness and uncertainty of the concrete instances of the boundaries. Humour protects us against inflexible and tyrannical orthodoxies.

Humour explores the boundaries of the acceptable.

Cultivating Rootedness:

A salient feature of our problem-solving culture is its disregard of our rootedness in the past — its disregard of soul. In reality we live in communication with the dead, who "live" by their influence on us. But by disregarding or denying this in our conscious life we disconnect consciousness from unconscious life and try to live as if life were identical with consciousness. This implies a self-definition that is confined to the present moment, a life that emerges from nothingness and vanishes again into nothingness — conditions for pursuing excitement or, if one is more serious-minded, being preoccupied with "existential *angst*".

Many people are currently searching for their ancestral roots, a desire that is intensified by the conditions just described. Their deeper roots are to be found in the soul — rootedness in the past of the entire universe. The best civilization would cultivate an awareness of the reality of the person as a permanent structure in temporal space extending as a para-structure into the entire universe and especially the human past.

Regaining our roots.

Our Roots in God:

Creation, Truth, and Beneficence are the patterns for the parental instinct and sociable love. The social animals are rooted in these patterns, so that rootedness in God is what distinguishes the social animals from other living things. (This, of course, is subject to degrees.) Notice that rootedness in Creation, Truth, and Beneficence (being similar to them **as patterns**) is not the same as the operation of Creation, Truth, and Beneficence on individual processes; the latter applies to all processes having any degree of individuality.

Rootedness in Creation, Truth, and Beneficence is primarily a set of tendencies due to the universe rather than due to consciousness. Ethics is a characteristic of consciousness, and if our rootedness in God is to be fully effective ethically, we need to cultivate a consciousness of Creation, Truth, and Beneficence as the ideal patterns to which ethical attitudes and conduct are analogous. Consequently, the best kind of culture will cultivate such a consciousness as well as the knowledge of the dependence of the good of its participants on ethics.

From Problem Solving to Cultivating Attitudes:

This brings us back to the theme of the introductory chapter. Our problem-solving civilization has an air of urgency and hurry due to the way in which solving problems generates other problems, eventually generating more problems and more serious problems than it solves. A culture of cultivating the best attitudes would shift attention from isolated situations to the global reality in which we must live. This would not entail neglecting **A culture of attitudes** details or the problems that genuinely need to be solved, since the principles of reality are common to all scales. Also, attitudes do not replace attention to details but rather govern the manner in which that attention is given. The important effect of a culture of attitudes would be that attention to problems would not mean neglecting global considerations.

Conceptions of the Desiderata:

In our problem-solving culture the tendency is to think of desiderata in focussed terms rather than in comprehensive terms. For example, the desiderata of the workplace are thought of as maximizing the output relative to the time workers spend on the job. This is in contrast with thinking of the desiderata of the workplace as maximizing the goods of the community in all categories.

What is wasting time?

This affects one's conception of what it is to waste time. If one were thinking in the former way, one might, for example, think nurses ought to work as hard as they can, and one might hire fewer nurses rather than more. This maximizes output relative to input. The fact that it leads to a higher frequency of mistakes and a degraded quality of patient care is not accounted for in this focussed conception of the desideratum. On the other hand, if time spent in a way that degrades the quality of life is understood as time wasted, one will hire more nurses at generous rates of pay and arrange for them to have adequate time to do their duties and also have time for visiting. This will minimize mistakes and minimize the loss of nurses to illness and disaffection. Which approach is more wasteful of time?

A culture aiming at cultivating the best attitudes would tend to think of desiderata in comprehensive rather than focussed terms. One would then zero in on particular issues in the light of the comprehensive conception of desiderata.

But How Do We Cultivate Good Attitudes?

This question is about education, especially education of the young. And I think it must depend on two factors:

1. Education on the principle of freedom: this gives young people the experience of being treated in the ethically best way, namely by having opportunities for maximizing their individuality prepared and administered for them.
2. Adults as patterns of good attitudes: without patterns of good attitudes, other means of inculcating good attitudes are subverted by the influence of examples that contradict the otherwise good effort. At the level of consciousness the inferior example says that they don't really mean what they say. However, this is too simple a statement. If we are to move to a better culture than we now have, we must help the younger generation to be better than we are. The example we set will therefore necessarily be inferior to the vision we set before them. But we must distinguish between the example of conduct and emotions and the example of attitudes. Attitudes are features of consciousness and can be adopted by choice. Young people are keenly sensitive to attitudes, and if they see that their would-be mentors have adopted attitudes that they are perhaps incapable of living up to, they will be forgiven their weakness and credited for their resolution.

But can we, as products of an inferior culture, take up a superior one?

The answer is that it begins with knowledge. Our culture is inferior in some ways to what we need, but it is strong in a tradition of seeking knowledge and setting a high value on knowledge. The key to transcending the conceptual limitations of one's culture is logic. The operation of denial makes it possible to entertain hypotheses incompatible with one's current culture. Logical reasoning makes it possible to extend one's thoughts beyond the scope of one's experience. Our very culture, which has cultivated logical reasoning and scientific investigation of hypotheses, has given us the means of transcending its conceptual limitations.

AFTERWORD: SOME IMPLICATIONS OF CRICHTON'S PHILOSOPHICAL SYSTEM FOR PSYCHOLOGY - BY CARL SEMMELROTH PH.D.

This foundational book, like the foundation for a building, determines the nature of the structures built upon it. Presented here are a few implications of Crichton's philosophical system for psychology.

As to its foundations, psychology today may be roughly divided into two parts. One part, represented by classical learning theory and its physiological relatives, American behaviorism, psychobiology, sensory psychophysics, and their cousins, finds its foundation in the harsh materialism of the physical sciences. Apart from these psychologies that claim materialism as a foundation are "all the rest." Cognitive psychologies, motivational psychologies, dynamic psychologies, and their cousins, claim no discernable foundation at all other than constructs that originate from everyday language use or constructs that emerge from the construction of psychological tests. Modern psychologists are left with a choice between standing on the rock of materialism and studying humans as one more aspect of a purely physical world, or studying humans by skipping deftly, like a logger on a river of logs, from one floating set of constructs to another, hoping to keep bits of psychological theory together and flowing.

Unfortunately, a choice between the rock of materialism and the river of floating constructs also implies a choice between including and excluding phenomena that are transcendent of the physical world. Materialistic psychology necessarily views the mind as the brain. Thinking is the brain acting as a computer. Feeling is limbic activity. Consciousness is an altered brain state. Each phenomenon refers to nothing more than its physical manifestation. And given its materialist foundation, nothing more can ever emerge from psychological theory. Unlike physics, where the physical reality of the chairs physicists sit on is no different than the reality of the chairs' atoms, materialist psychologists can never make *their* conscious experiences out of nerve impulses, and keep both as real. No wonder so many psychologists have chosen the river. There, although their footing is without foundation, they need not sacrifice the reality of their consciousness.

At the beginning of Chapter 4, Crichton boldly stakes out a foundation that will accommodate experience along with material particles in a coherent view of nature that includes more than elementary particles.

"How do you begin to develop a deeper understanding of nature than that which science has already given us? You need a notion of the **elements** of reality. Physics gives us a notion of the elements as being the **elementary particles**. But reality is more than **things**; it is also events or changes, and also the underlying causes of these.

"Elements must be both irreducible and comprehensive, and they must together comprise all of reality. This implies that they cover both the parts and the whole, as well as intermediate wholes and how all these work together.

"I propose that **structure, change** and **tendency** are genuine elements of reality, at least some of them. Structure and change are material, but tendency, although affecting material things, may not be entirely material; it may have an ingredient that transcends time and space."

Why is this important? Crichton states in a deceptively simple statement at the beginning of Chapter 5 why basing his analysis on the elementary categories of structure, change, and tendency provides conclusions that apply to psychology as well as physics:

"Structure, change, and tendency are not only present in all levels of scale and organization but are exemplified in all of them as well. Not only does a human community have structures in it, but it is itself a structure. Changes are the same kind of thing whether they happen to molecules or human bodies or international relations. Tendencies are the same kind of thing whether they are the tendencies of molecules or of human bodies or of international relations. Thus, holistic and mechanistic causality are brought under the same principles, principles that not only apply at all levels but bring all levels together under these same principles. And there is no gulf between the topics of physics and chemistry and those of psychology and ethics, but all are just variant applications of the same principles."

Crichton's proofs concerning the tendencies of natural events are carried out without recourse to explanations that depend on "natural laws" that science assumes as "super-natural" rulers of physical events. He is able to place causation within an entirely natural framework. Natural "laws" are evolving as part of nature. They aren't **super**-natural. The naturalistic existence of tendency reveals the inseparable connection between consciousness, creation, and change. Natural existence includes both conscious experiences and atoms.

His system is pregnant with psychological theories, like a queen bee is pregnant with a multitude of related offspring, each carrying the same genetic signature, but doing different work while living together in the same hive.

A few of the offspring are likely to be in the areas of psychological health, the nature and importance of relationships, and the reality and usefulness of our feelings as our awareness of our tendencies. Crichton's on-going proofs, premised only on the existence of structure, change, and tendency, lead to conclusions concerning health and relationships. These are woven into his deductions concerning what it means to be individuated as a being.

An example of the Crichton's revelations concerning health is the connection he reveals between individuality, well-being, freedom, and what he call's "vivacity" – behavior in the living present that contributes to well-being - see page 37.   He emphasizes that in addition to well-being health is functioning that contributes to well-being, that is, it is functioning that contributes to our individualities - our wholeness and distinctiveness. This consists of functioning of subsystems of the body and of external relationships such that they contribute to our individualities. Especially important to our individualities are our relationships. They are literally part of our individualities because of what Crichton calls "complementation."

Health is both living that produces well-being, as well as well-being itself. In turn, our way of living, because it is more or less well patterned, has more or less distinctiveness and wholeness. Therefore the way we promote our well-being, itself has more or less well-being. So health includes the living of our lives in ways that *produce* wholeness and distinctiveness of us as persons, not just the state of being whole and distinct as persons.

This forms a bridge to a coherent view of freedom and its relationship to individualities of persons - see page 126 and following. After pointing out the usually noticed limitations of frequent historical treatments of freedom as either "absence of restrains vs. opportunity," he uses the foundations he has built for understanding individuality and health to take the idea of freedom in a novel direction. He agrees that freedom is opportunity, but asks, "Opportunity for what?" He derives the ideal of freedom as "maximum opportunity to maximize one's vivacity." Thus he uses the derivation of "vivacity" - living in ways that increase well-being – to illuminate what individual freedom is and what it's good for. He proceeds to explicate what "opportunity" for maximizing one's actual living so it contributes to one's well-being. Sociable love provides a social environment that contributes dependable social structures that circumscribe and make perceptible opportunities for increasing vivacity.

The implications for psychology of Crichton's analysis of freedom are numerous. Among the implications is a change of focus concerning mental health from just a state of well-being, to inclusion of the manner in which one lives. Mentally healthy living involves freely acting on opportunities for increasing well-being. In addition, Crichton explicates the importance of a social environment that includes dependable structures and circumscribed opportunities for freedom to operate. He even includes the fine arts as an important part of what he calls a "freedom culture."

And one cannot leave his contribution to understanding the importance of social structures without underlining the central role of what he calls "sociable love." Sociable love ties the well-being of others into our own well-being. Sociable love does not mean "love of community." Rather it refers to our love that is patterned after the parental instinct. It is our tendency to view the well-being of others in the same way as our own. It applies not only to other people whose well-being is important to one, but to all of our concerns over any object's well-being, perhaps a painting, a flowering plant in the garden, a mathematical proof, a tree, or even a book or an ideology.

Because Crichton's discovery of the nature of causality by patterns, is key to many psychological implications of his work, perhaps it is worth reviewing it.

The metaphor of an incomplete jigsaw puzzle, although misleading in some respects, helps us to get at the nature of causality and its relationship to feelings.

Picture a jigsaw puzzle whose entire edge is unfinished. The puzzle represents every physical state of the material universe since its beginning up to the present moment. That is, each piece of the puzzle represents a single change that occurred since the center piece appeared at the formation of the first physical particle preceding the "big bang." A mighty big puzzle! In addition, there is a creator of the puzzle that is responsible for creating each material piece from the beginning. Because this creator of material particles existed prior to all structure, tendencies, and changes, it cannot itself have any of these attributes. It has no intelligence, no material existence, and no structure of any kind. Because it has no structure of its own, the creator's awareness of the puzzle can only be exactly what the puzzle is and the shapes of pieces can only affect the shape of the new pieces it creates already there. This may sound harshly restrictive on the creator, but it is similar to the position you are in as a jig saw puzzle solver. You cannot plan what the puzzle will look like and you are restricted to adding only pieces that fit with what is already there. The creative factor's awareness consists only of an exact awareness of everything about the puzzle – the shape of every piece, the shape of each combination of pieces taken one at a time, two at a time, three at a time etc., and the direction and distance of each piece from every other piece. Therefore, included in its awareness is the puzzle's edge. Because it creates and its awareness is inclusive of everything existing, the puzzle's creator "sees" the relationships between the shapes of all the existing pieces and the edge of the puzzle. Similarities between what exists and the shape of the edge determine what is possible to create at any given time. Because the puzzle's creator has no existence other than creative awareness, it does not exist in any location that could ever be included in the puzzle. This is to say, it has no material relationship to the puzzle. It is literally nowhere in space. Its relationship to the puzzle is only through awareness/creation. So it is equally aware of everything about the puzzle.

The puzzle plus its transcendent creator include all existence, all of nature. The puzzle contains all of material creation since the beginning of the material universe and all the precedents that cause what comes next. All existence is still there in its material form. The edge of the puzzle is what exists in the present; it is the present everywhere in the universe. Starting from the first piece ever created, if you were to count outward toward the edge, the present, you will have counted time, all time. All material change that has ever occurred or will occur is creation at the edge of what exists and adds to it.

Like all metaphors, this "flat world" picture leaves out a good deal. For example it is in two-space. Also it implies that created patterns literally touch one another in space, as do the jigsaw puzzle pieces. It is the individuation of patterns of matter due to relationships that is represented metaphorically by the puzzle pieces. Unlike puzzle pieces, fundamental particles are separated by space. Furthermore, our imaginations begin to fail as we try to expend the puzzle pieces laid out before us into three dimensions and then try to imagine the addition of pieces in a fourth dimension, time, so that the outer edge is present time. If we were able to imagine the entire history of the material universe in four dimensions, we would see the shape of the outside surface as the limiting possibilities for what can happen next. The future is limited, at any time, to those patterns that most resemble patterns already existing inside that most easily lock onto the surface shapes. The present literally has a material shape. Shapes existing in the past, any place and any time in the universe, that have resemblances to something that would fit with the shape of the present, constitute the active tendencies for change in the present. Such is the nature of causation proposed by Crichton.

What has this to do with feelings? Crichton's theory of consciousness is that individual consciousness is an individual's participation in the creator's awareness, except a person's awareness is limited to one's local position in space-time. The creator's awareness is of all potential fits of the past to present circumstances. Therefore, our feelings are our awareness of causal tendencies that are operating on local possibilities, mainly our bodies. Thus, a potentially close fit of any pattern existing anywhere in the history of the universe to one's present circumstance could be experienced as a feeling and could constitute a tendency for one's behavior. However, patterns existing in our own history or the histories of persons or other animals like us are likely to furnish closer fits and therefore become more frequent as exemplars for our behaviors.

The implications of this are vast. What of Jung's collective unconscious? Could his archetypes be representations of deep natural tendencies? Is there a naturalistic explanation for the effects of myth? What are the possibilities for a deep understanding of our lives extending back beyond those who raised us to those whose lives serve as patterns from afar in space-time? Can we cultivate our sensitivity to subtle feelings to the point where we can detect enormously more possibilities for our behaviors in any given circumstance?

I am reminded of four students who came to me many years ago with a proposal for a natural observation "experiment" concerning feelings. They proposed keeping diaries of all their feelings, recorded every ten minutes of wake-time for a week. In preparation for their recordings, they tried to prepare an exhaustive list of human feelings. The list started with a few dozen feelings and quickly got out of hand. **Crichton's work implies that a complete list of feelings could never have been completed by them, which itself has implications for our notions of science of human behaviors.** According to this work there is potentially a feeling for every behavior of which we are capable, that is, for every precedent existing in space time that bears any resemblance to present circumstance. There is a tendency influencing our behavior, potentially accessible by us as a feeling, originating from every pattern in the history of the universe that bears some resemblance to our present circumstance.

The potential influence of the system presented in this book on all areas of psychology is enormous. The examples of its treatment of feelings, well-being, individuality, health, and freedom are only a sample. Many of us who have toiled a lifetime in the psychology garden have tired of growing barren plants, plants that resist our attempt to make them bear fruits expected of materialistic science, a botanical family that is not their own. Crichton's work cultivates the ground for another kind of garden, an exciting place where science and mind can blossom together. The soil provided by Crichton's philosophical system is rich and firm. It awaits a thoroughly naturalistic psychology to take root.

APPENDIX A – FOUNDATIONS: THE ARGUMENT

The procedure here is, first to define the elements (change, structure, and tendency) on the basis of experience, then to determine by logic what their necessary properties are and what the ontological implications of their existence are.

The argument here has the premise that these elements exist, only that. The meaning and also verification of that premise depends on defining these elements on the basis of experience.

What is experience? Experience is observation, but it is more than observation of things and events. It is the history of one's consciousness. To be fully informed by experience one must observe one's experience, that is, one must observe one's consciousness and the record of experience in memory. It is possible to observe one's consciousness because of the possibility of special points of view.[42]

Theory does not test experience.

Evidence is experience. There is a tendency, whenever a theory or an opinion has acquired the status of orthodoxy, to give it a status that belongs to experience. It is acknowledged that theory is tested by experience, not experience by theory, but people often do not adhere to that principle and instead declare certain experiences to be non-existent or illusory or delusive if accepted theories have no place for them. Therefore, it is important to emphasize here that **theories are not evidence for or against experience; experience is evidence for or against theories**.

---

[42]See "Objectivity" in " Consciousness, Choice, & Reasoning".

1. The Nature of Change:

There are two sources of confusion about the nature of change and about past, present, and future. One is the fact that what we perceive by our bodily senses is only the present moment. This makes it appear that what is past has ceased to exist and only what is in the present moment exists.

The other is the theory of relativity, which gives the impression that before and after, past and future, are artifacts of the circumstances of observation and vary with those circumstances. (But this is a misinterpretation. It is the **measurements** of these things that vary with those circumstances.)

Pay attention to experience.

Now, both common sense and science tell us that the first principle of gaining knowledge is to pay careful attention to experience. Most of us, scientists included, are seldom as meticulous in adhering to this principle as we might be. But let us see what experience tells us about change. **What do we all know when we are not thinking about science or philosophy?**

I think of the case of a PhD candidate about to take the oral examination for the dissertation. PhD students have invested heavily for high stakes, at least the stakes look very high to them. A student about to take the oral examination is keenly aware that passing the examination is something that has not yet happened and possibly may never happen. A student who has just taken the oral examination and been congratulated on success is keenly aware that passing the examination is something that has happened and can never fail to have happened.

This is an example of special interest to academics. But we can all think of events important in our own lives that illustrate the same vivid awareness of the difference between past and future.

- ❑ We know that what has happened is a real event that will always be a real event in the past and can never fail to be a real event in the past.
- ❑ We know that what has not yet happened is not a real event and may never be one.

Real events happen only to real things.

- ❑ Thus, the past is the domain of real events, and the future is the domain of merely possible events.

So much for events, you say. But the **things** that existed in the past and have been destroyed, like a house that has burned to the ground — these have ceased to exist.

What about this? Allowing that it is true in one obvious sense, namely that they are no longer present in the present, is it true in the deeper sense that the things that once existed in the present **no longer exist in the past?** Does "in the past" imply "nonexistent"? Or do things in the past **still exist in the past?**

- ❑ Events or changes happen to things, to structure.
- ❑ Events are defined, not only by their position in time but by their content, that is, what was changed by them.

If things cease to exist, so do events.

- ❑ Therefore, if the things to which events once occurred cease to exist, the events also are reduced to nothing (although it was the case that the candidate passed the exam, it has become the case that he or she did not pass it).
- ❑ Therefore, if things in the past are not real now, neither are the events that happened to them.
- ❑ But events in the past are still real, as we showed above (the candidate really did pass the exam).

Things that once existed still exist in the past.

- ❑ Therefore, things that once existed in the present are now real things in the past.

How is this possible? It is possible because of **temporal space.**

- ❑ Events happen to things in space.
- ❑ Therefore, those things are still in space.
- ❑ If they are still in space, but are not here and now, then they must exist somewhere else in space.
- ❑ That "somewhere else" must be in the past.

Enduring things are processes in temporal space.

- ❑ Therefore, space must have a temporal dimension as well as the three dimensions perceptible by the bodily senses.

❑ That is, space is temporal space (space-time in the language of physics).

❑ Things that endure through time (rocks, trees, people) are processes in temporal space — structures being extended in the temporal dimension of temporal space. When they go out of existence in the everyday sense, they come to an end in the temporal dimension, but the complete process— the completed structure — continues to exist in the past of temporal space.

Change is extension of structure.

What is said about things here applies to their properties as well, for the same reasons. Thus, nothing ever ceases to exist. This tells us what the nature of change is. Change does not remove anything from existence, neither things nor their properties. The only remaining alternative is that change brings something new into existence, a new element of structure. **Change is extension of structure.**

This would also be the reasonable inference from the concept of space-time in physics, but physicists appear to have continued to think in 3-dimensional terms, thinking of change as replacement of the state at a given place or of a given entity changing location. But their own diagrams representing space-time present a different conception.

2. The Discreteness of Change & Structure:

Change is not strictly continuous but occurs in minimum steps, and structures are composed of separate minimal structural elements — particles. Physics discovered this empirically in the 20th Century, but in the present context it has to be demonstrated, and I begin with the discreteness of change.

Proof that Change Is Discrete

In Greece, a generation or two before Socrates, Zeno of Elea put forward several arguments to show that continuous motion (motion that traversed the entire space between the starting and finishing positions, thus that went through an infinite number of positions between any two positions) was impossible. In philosophy courses, these arguments are usually presented as arguments against the possibility of motion without qualification and are therefore presented as "paradoxes". But historically they were part of a larger difference of opinion as between discrete and continuous conceptions of material reality, Plato's school championing discreteness and Aristotle's school championing continuity.

Aristotle, a few generations after Zeno, argued against Zeno's arguments[43], defending continuity of motion and change in general. Aristotle was not unskilled in logic, but his reasoning in this case was distorted by prejudice — it was important to him to think of the motion of the stars as the image of divinity, and for this to satisfy his notion of perfection, that motion had to be continuous — unbroken. A succession of distinct states, even if infinitely interspersed, would not satisfy him. (This prejudice had unfortunate consequences for the history of science, but still, I cannot help liking him for having it. There may be more important things than getting ontology right.)

Aristotle's **stated** reason for thinking Zeno's arguments were ineffective is a useful vehicle for showing that Zeno was right and that change is discrete.

One of Zeno's arguments (my formulation):

Change from a given state cannot begin, since to begin is to proceed immediately to another state, but it cannot proceed immediately to any

To begin it must have already begun.

particular state because it must first proceed to an intermediate state. And then you can argue in the same way that it cannot proceed to *that* state. Or to put it a little differently, to change to **any** state it must have **already** changed to another state. **To begin it must have already begun**.

Aristotle points out that Zeno can argue in this way because he thinks of change as merely the occurrence of another state, with nothing happening between the two states. In that case **any actual change is the immediate occurrence of another state**.

Against this Aristotle says that states do not connect states in time, just as points on a line do not connect points (even if they are densely ordered.) A line connects points. Therefore, if change is only the occurrence of another state, it does not connect the state **from** which to the state **to** which the change takes place. Aristotle says that

Zeno: Change is only the occurrence of another state.

Aristotle: Change is something happening between states.

---

[43]In *Physics* Book VI mainly, also in Book VIII.

change (Greek **kinesis,** or movement) is what connects states. States are separated by time, and that time is covered by the change from state to state. So change is something different from the states that it connects, and like the time between states, it is continuous.

The crucial point in answer to Aristotle is that change must make a difference; it must bring new states; a "change" that does not change anything is not a change. To say that there is continuous change from one actual state to the next actual state but no difference of actual states during that time is to say that the change does not change anything, **except for being the occurrence of the new state at the end of that time** (but this is Zeno's view).

A change must make a change.

Aristotle invokes his distinction between potential and actual to forestall this objection, treating **kinesis** as containing a series of **potential** states. However, only actual states are real states, and only actual changes are real changes. "Changes" to merely potential states do not change anything and are therefore not changes but only potential changes. This is the same as saying that something else **might** have happened then, although it did not. Consequently, Aristotle's notion of continuous **kinesis** between distinct states is empty and reduces to discrete change between those endpoint states.

Aristotle **almost** admits that if change is only the occurrence of new states, then Zeno's argument holds: to begin is to have already begun, but to have begun before beginning is a contradiction. We may state Zeno's argument in another way that may make it more transparent:

A change is nothing but the occurrence of a new state.

If change is only the occurrence of new states, then a change from a given state must be one of the following:

1. The occurrence of no state.
2. The occurrence of just one state.
3. The occurrence of two or more successive states simultaneously.
4. The occurrence of two or more simultaneous states.
5. The occurrence of an undifferentiated succession of states.

#1 is no change at all. #3 is self-contradictory. In #4 the states make up a single state, since they are simultaneous. Then #5 would either be the same as #2, because undifferentiated states are really just one state, or else it would be equivalent to Aristotle's *kinesis*, which we have seen to be vacuous. So we are left with #2 as the only possibility.

In other words, change is discrete.

Change is discrete.

This is also the view that physics was forced to adopt in the 20th Century. What I have shown is that what the empirical evidence shows is in fact logically necessary.

What about Structure?

A change is the occurrence of a new state of structure. The change is the same as what is new about the new state. Therefore, the properties of what is new about the new state are the properties of the change.

There are minimal changes, changes that are strictly single, with no smaller changes within them — no distinction of parts within them.

Structure is discrete.

Therefore, what is new about the new state of structure has no distinction of parts within it. It is a minimal element of structure — a particle in the strict sense.

In other words, structure is discrete.

3. One Change at a Time:

Changes are simply ordered, not partially ordered. That is, only one minimal change occurs at a time in the universe — not just locally, but in the universe.

This is contrary to common sense. Common sense tells us that changes are going on simultaneously all around. But common sense is based on the bodily senses, which are not sensitive to minimal changes but treat long sequences of minimal changes as simultaneous. Certainly, in terms of time scales of a tenth of a second or more, changes are simultaneous throughout the universe. But the question here is about minimal changes.

Then it is thought that relativity theory implies that simultaneity is not even exactly defined at distances from any point at which measurements are taken. This is true in terms of measurements. Measurements are affected by relative motion, which is the point of relativity theory. But measurements occur at the point at which measurements are taken, not at the distant point of what is measured. This should tell us that relativity theory (the special theory is at issue here) is not about what is actually there in the universe, but about the dynamics of measurement.

The thesis here is that the partial ordering of minimal events is logically inconsistent.

- ❏ We have seen that a minimal event is the creation of a particle.
- ❏ If minimal changes are partially ordered, there will be instances of two particles such that neither of them was created before the other, in other words the order of the times of their creation is not defined.
- ❏ Let X and Y be two such particles. Then, at the time of the coming into existence of X, it is undefined whether Y exists or not.
- ❏ But this is impossible. Y either exists or does not exist. It cannot both exist and not exist, nor can it neither exist nor not exist, nor can it "sort of" exist but not really. What is there in the universe is definitely there, and what is not there is definitely not there.

Therefore, minimal changes are simply ordered, and just one particle is created at a time in the universe.

4. Transcendence:

The question for this section is this: is it possible that tendencies are due to structure and its past changes **and nothing else**? Or do tendencies depend on a transcendent factor, something not in space and time?

Another way of expressing the question is this: Is there a cause of events that is not in time at all, or are all the causes of events also events (or the results of events) that precede their effects in time?

The principle here is this: If causes that precede their effects in time are to be effective, something must connect those causes to the potentialities for those effects. Otherwise, the effects are separated from their causes. And if the effects are detached from their causes, the causes can have no effect on them.

This is because a cause that occurs in time and space can act only where and when it occurs. Later would be when it is no longer active.

A cause can act only when it occurs, not later.

- ❏ Now suppose that the only basis for tendencies is existing structure and its past changes.
- ❏ Structure itself as such is inert. It must be the changes to structure that can act as causes.
- ❏ But the changes are earlier than their hypothetical effects and cannot act later than they occur. (This is the principle behind the doctrine of "no action at a distance".)
- ❏ Therefore, neither the structure nor the changes to structure can be effective as causes by themselves.

- ❑ Therefore, tendencies cannot be based on changing structure alone.[44]
- ❑ However, there are real tendencies.
- ❑ Therefore, tendencies must be based on something in addition to changing structure, outside the category of structure and change.
- ❑ Being outside the category of structure and change, this additional factor is devoid of structure and incapable of changing.
- ❑ And it must be able to connect the past cause to the future potential effect so as to make the material cause an effective cause of that effect.
- ❑ To do this it must produce the effect in response to existing structure and its history of changes. Any other way of connecting them would fail to make the material cause an effective cause of that effect.

An actuating factor, not in space or time

- ❑ Not being in space and time, it is at no distance (either zero or positive) from either the causes or the effects. Consequently, it is unaffected by the principle that causes can act only where and when they are.

I call this additional factor the **creative factor**.

5. One Creative Factor & One Universe:

There is only one creative factor and one universe, and that universe is the domain of that one creative factor. The argument for this is as follows:

1. There are not two or more creative factors creating the same events.
   - ❑ A single action is the action of a single agent. Two unconnected agents have distinct actions.
   - ❑ If there were two or more creative factors in the same universe, they would be the same as one creative factor with a structure, since the common action would connect them.
   - ❑ But the creative factor has no structure.
   - ❑ Therefore, a given series of events is created by just one creative factor.

This includes the history of the universe.

2. The history of the universe is a single, sequential act of the creative factor.

---

[44]This argument up to this point was first put forward by David Hume in the 18th Century, and its validity is one of the few things nearly all philosophers agree on.

- ❏ The change to a given state was an extension of the preceding state of structure.
- ❏ Therefore, the creative factor did not effectuate the given state independently of the preceding state.
- ❏ Therefore, when the creative factor effectuated the given state, it was responding to the preceding state.
- ❏ That preceding state was an extension of the state preceding it.

All the changes are one sequential action.

- ❏ Therefore, by the same argument, the creative factor was responding to that earlier state, and by the same argument to all earlier states. Thus, the creative factor is always responding to the entire history of the universe.
- ❏ If an action is a response to a preceding action by the same agent, they are a single sequential action.
- ❏ Therefore, the history of the universe is a single sequential action of the creative factor.

3.   There are not two or more independent universes with different creative factors, only one.

- ❏ If there were two, they would have independent sequences of changes.
- ❏ If their respective times were related as earlier and later, the two sequences would not be independent.
- ❏ Therefore, their respective times would not be related as earlier and later.
- ❏ But this is impossible, because consider two particles X in one universe and Y in the other. At the time when X comes into existence the time when Y comes into existence would be neither earlier nor later nor the same. Otherwise the sequences of changes would not be independent. Therefore, at the time when X comes into existence it would be undefined whether Y existed or not.

One universe

- ❏ But existence cannot be undefined. A particle cannot both exist and not exist, nor can it neither exist nor not exist, nor can it exist but not really. It must either definitely exist or definitely not exist. This is true at every time. (Recall that times are defined by what exists. Existence, not time, is primitive. Therefore, offering different conceptions of time cannot circumvent the argument.)

❑ Therefore, there are not two or more independent universes.

Physicists and philosophers are enamoured of a "many-universes" interpretation of quantum theory, the idea being that an infinity of alternative universes actually exists. This seems to me to be a failure to distinguish potentiality from actuality. I cannot comment on quantum theory from a physicist's point of view, but it would seem to me that quantum theory is about the potential events under given conditions and their probabilities. But just as mathematicians seem to overlook the fact that mathematics is about possibilities and necessities, not actualities, so physicists have recently entertained as ontologically possible hypotheses that most of them some years ago would have scorned as nonsense in physical terms. In the "post-modern" spirit there seems to be a growing willingness to eliminate the distinction between representations and the represented realities, or to allow that all possible concepts refer to realities. It is only a step from there to allowing that logical contradictions can describe peculiar realities; after all, Lewis Carroll's tales have a certain plausibility, which arises as soon as one suspends this connection between logic and semantics. This is a dangerous trend, because nature is unaffected by such fashions and will not save us from the consequences of playing loosely with logic and semantics.

4. There was a first event.
  ❑ There is a structure that has been created by the creative factor.
  ❑ That structure was created by a single (though sequential) act of the creative factor.[45]
  ❑ That being the case, the agent that performed that action must have existed before doing so, since an agent must first exist in order to perform an action. Therefore, the creative factor existed before creating that structure, therefore before that structure existed at all, therefore before any part of it existed, therefore before any changes had occurred.
  ❑ But change is discrete.
  ❑ Therefore, the changes could begin only with a single change.   **A beginning of change**
  ❑ That is to say, **there was a first change, a first event.**
  ❑ Objection: The changes might extend infinitely into the past,

---

[45]See above, #2.

and the creative factor might have existed before each minimal change.

❑ Reply: This ignores the theorem that what was created was a single structure by a single action. To perform a single action, the creative factor must exist before that action is performed.

5. There was no structure existing before the first event.

For "before the first event" to be meaningful, the hypothetical structure would have to be part of this same universe and created by the same creative factor.

But then there would have been other events before the first event, which is a contradiction. **This proves the theorem.**

6. There is only one creative factor and one universe, dynamically united under that one creative factor.

❑ We are given that there are not two or more independent universes, that there was a first event, that there **One creative factor, one universe, dynamically united** was no uncreated structure existing before that first event, and that all events form a single action resulting in a single structure.

❑ That is to say, there is only one creative factor and one universe, dynamically united under that one creative factor.

At this point the reader may have a sceptical question pending since the beginning of Appendix A, namely, how is it possible to reach universal conclusions on the basis of existential premises?

❑ If that had been done by a process of generalization, it would obviously be deductively invalid, or could have no more than probability.

❑ But one may verify that no steps of generalization have been made. Instead, I have followed a process of restricting the scope of existence within certain specified bounds, in other words, a process of elimination. For example, no partial ordering of events, no structure before the first event, no multiplicity of creative factors. This results in universal conclusions, but in the form of saying that **only such-and-such a universe exists.**

6. All Structures Are Spatial:

Every structure is created by the one creative factor, and the creative factor creates only structures in temporal space. Therefore, all structures are spatial. This implies that conceptual structures, for example, insofar as they are structures rather than para-structures, do not take some mysterious immaterial form but are really spatial structures in temporal space. In many cases they are embodied in things like printing on paper or the sounds of speech. In other cases they are representations in one's brain, which are structures in temporal space. That is, their development over time leaves a structure stretched out in the temporal dimension of temporal space.

7. Empty Space Is Continuous:

Consider the position of a new particle as the extension of a process. It has many possible positions, and there is no minimum distance separating them. That is, the possible positions are densely distributed, in other words the space is continuous.

8. Tendencies Are Not Deterministic:

At any time there are many different active tendencies, and these correspond to possible extensions of processes. Since these are all possible, no one of them is predetermined to occur. In other words, tendencies are not deterministic.

9. Structural Complementation:

What a particle is: Are the spatial relations of a particle with other particles an aspect of the particle, or is the body of the particle the complete particle?

- ❏ If the body of the particle were the complete particle, its spatial relations would be distinct entities and not merely the relations of the particle. They would really be other particles. The particle would then have another set of relations relating it to its own spatial relations. But in that case its spatial relations would not really be its relations.

The complete particle includes its structural relations.

- ❏ Therefore, the spatial relations must be an aspect of what the particle is. The body of the particle is **complemented** by its spatial relations. The complete particle is the **complemented** body of the particle. This is the principle of **structural complementation**.

- ❑ This is reflected in the fact that when a new particle is created, it is created not merely as a body but as an element of a structure, with all its structural relations with other particles.
- ❑ Those structural relations are then imposed on all other particles, so that a particle acquires new structural relations with each subsequent creation of a particle. Thus, what a given particle is altered by each subsequent creation of a particle.
- ❑ The same argument applies to individual things and their relations in general, so that what a thing is includes its relations with other individual things.
- ❑ However, compound structures and processes are different from particles in this way, that whereas a particle is unambiguously a definite single thing, a compound structure or process is only a definite single thing to the degree that it has individuality.
- ❑ Therefore, for compound structures and processes, what they are includes those relations with other things **that contribute to their individuality.**

10. Causality by Patterns:

The creative factor takes the specification of tendencies from what is in temporal space. This must be so, since transcendent tendencies are impossible.

The question is, how can the creative factor do this?

- ❑ The creative factor has no transcendent structure. Therefore, it cannot process information from the material world the way we do, forming a constructed perception. It can only sense the world exactly as it is.

The creative factor senses the world exactly as it is.

- ❑ The specification of the tendencies must be present in the material world just as it is.
- ❑ Therefore, the only way in which what is in temporal space can bias the creative factor is by being what it is. **What is there must contain the patterns for what is to be there.**
- ❑ That is, the patterns actually present in temporal space must be the patterns for potential extensions of structure.
- ❑ In general, a given process cannot be extended **exactly** following a given pattern, if only because their locations are not the same.
- ❑ Therefore, that bias must be **the similarity between patterns in temporal space and potential extensions of structure.**

- ❑ The creative factor "sees" the patterns in the spatial extensions of processes. This is the same as saying the creative factor is conscious of the similarity between them. Then the comparative intensity of "seeing" a pattern is the bias towards creating an extension similar to that pattern.
- ❑ That intensity and bias will be stronger the more instances of the given pattern there are.
- ❑ Therefore, the tendency of a process to resemble a given pattern is greater
  - ○ The greater the similarity between the potential extension and that pattern, and
  - ○ The more instances of that pattern there are (the greater is its *prevalence*).

This is summarized by saying that:

The tendency of a specific potential extension (its tendency to resemble a given pattern) is its similarity to the pattern times the prevalence of the pattern.

Tendency = Similarity x Prevalence

A QUESTION: How do you know that the creative factor responds to the past history of structure? Maybe it only responds to the current state of structure, which is more like the view of modern physics.

The creative factor responds to the entire history of the universe.

- ❑ The answer was given above. The history of the universe is a single sequential act of the creative factor.

Thus, the creative factor is always responding to the entire history of the universe. This means that all the things and properties of things throughout the universe and throughout its history are patterns for future potentialities.

11. The Necessary Patterns:

The patterns are instances of structure, change, and tendency. There are a number of logically necessary properties of structure, change, and tendency — the properties whose hypothetical alternatives are inconsistent with the defining properties of those elements as found in experience.

The necessary patterns (necessarily) occur in all instances of structure, change, and tendency, therefore in everything in the material universe and in every change and outcome of change.

This ensures that the universe and everything in it has certain properties. But can these necessary patterns be significant **as patterns for causality by**

patterns? If they occur by necessity, they cannot occur because of similarity — necessity pre-empts tendency.

This is true. But what **can** occur by similarity to the necessary patterns are changes and structures **analogous** to the necessary patterns.

For example, Permanence, the property of every structure and change of never going out of existence, has an analogue in the repetitiveness of a process (the endurance of its pattern over time). Thus, processes tend to be repetitive through similarity to this necessary pattern. Things tend to endure through time.

The necessary patterns have very great prevalence. Thus, everything tends to be analogous to the necessary patterns.

Then that tendency results in everything tending to be *closely* analogous to the necessary patterns, or to many of them.

The effect is that the product, **similarity x prevalence**, is very high.

The necessary patterns are the permanent core of nature.

12. Combined Patterns & Wholeness of Similarity:

There is an important class of patterns in consciousness, which I will call **special patterns**, the familiar cases being events in one's consciousness which have a very powerful effect on one's tendencies. Not all patterns in consciousness have this efficacy; many go by and are forgotten. I will call these **ordinary patterns**. As patterns, special patterns have little prevalence in consciousness, being unique events. How, then, can they have such a powerful effect on later events?

The question is why a special pattern gives the current potentiality so much potency. For example, the telephone rings and we feel compelled to answer it.

This is because the call may pertain to our important interests, interests vital to our individuality. This makes the ringing of the telephone by association[46] an instance of individuality, which has a very high prevalence in one's consciousness. And that makes the ringing of the telephone combine with individuality as a single pattern. This has wholeness of similarity to the potentiality.

That single pattern has a prevalence in consciousness equal to the sum of the prevalences of its component patterns and a similarity to the potentiality equal to the average of their similarities (which are essentially equal since the special pattern is an instance of the general pattern). **The high prevalence of the general pattern (individuality) gives the combined pattern a high prevalence and the potentiality a high potency.**

---

[46]See next section.

An ordinary pattern in consciousness does not have this effect of making the ordinary pattern combine with a pattern of high prevalence as a single pattern.

Consequently, it does not give the potentiality high potency.   Many elements of consciousness pass us by with little notice or effect in this way.

13. Tendency by Association:

Example: One hears the word "tree" and consequently thinks of trees. Yet the word "tree" has no significant similarity to a tree. What is the dynamic of causation due to association?

Two principles:

- ❏ To be similar is to be similar in some respects, not necessarily in all respects. Therefore, to be similar in some respects is to be similar. For example, a black stone and a black automobile are to that extent similar. (The degree of similarity is limited by the degree to which the aspect represents the concrete entity.)
- ❏ Therefore, similarity is transitive. If X is similar to Y, and Y is similar to Z, X is similar to Z (to some degree).

The argument, then, is as follows:

- ❏ One experiences trees in association with the word "tree" (being taught the meaning of the word).
- ❏ The subsequent experience of the word "tree" is similar to the experience of the associated pair.
- ❏ And the subsequent experience of trees is similar to the associated pair.
- ❏ Result: Seeing trees is a special pattern similar to the pattern of the associated pair.
- ❏ The latter pattern is potentially similar to an extension of the personal process. Therefore, there is a potential extension similar to it. Thus, seeing trees elicits the memory of the word "tree".
- ❏ Similarly, hearing the word "tree" elicits the memory of the associated pair.
- ❏ The memory of the associated pair is similar to the experience of trees.
- ❏ Therefore, there is a potentiality for thinking of trees.
- ❏ Thus, hearing the word "tree" elicits the thought of trees.

14. Tendencies as Patterns:

Tendencies in the past are no longer active, no longer efficacious as tendencies. But we have the principle that nothing ever goes out of existence. Does the case of tendencies violate that principle? And if not, can tendencies be significant patterns?

❏ Past tendencies are blocked from realization in the present, either by their own realization in the past or by the realization of other tendencies. It is important to think of this graphically, in terms of temporal space. The blocking is the occupation by particles of the space that constituted the potentiality.

❏ Otherwise the conditions relating potentialities to patterns remain in temporal space.

❏ This is because the history of the universe is preserved in the response of the creative factor to each new state. This implies that past potentialities and their comparison with patterns existing at that time are preserved in the creative factor's response to present states.

❏ As patterns for similar tendencies, do they make them more potent?

❏ To make them more potent requires a pattern similar to the potentiality.

❏ A past tendency would be similar to the potentiality, in that the past potentiality and its comparison with patterns at the time is similar to present potentialities and their comparison with patterns.

❏ Therefore, past tendencies are effective patterns for present potentialities.

15. Abstraction in Elementary Nature:

Two things are generally more similar in some respects than in others. Thus similarity distinguishes different properties of things. The necessary patterns, for example, are singled out by the fact that every instance of structure, change, or tendency is exactly similar to every other instance **in that respect** and less similar in other respects. This is abstraction.

Thus, abstraction is built in to the fabric of nature. It is not a pure human invention but has patterns in elementary nature.

APPENDIX B – NECESSARY PRECEDENTS: NECESSARY PATTERNS & THEIR ANALOGUES

THE NECESSARY PRECEDENTS
The necessary patterns are derived from the argument of Appendix A.
I will list a number of patterns under each category and then describe the patterns and some analogues.

IN THE CATEGORY OF PARTICLES

Necessary Patterns	Analogues
Particles	individuality
No Distinction of Parts	wholeness
Body	wholeness of form
Structural Complementation	interactional complementation protons & electrons atomic structure
Surrounding Relations Correspondence (relations & relata)	branched processes electric charge cognitive representations
Contrast (particle/space)	contrast in structures & processes

Particles: Each minimal change is the creation of a particle. A particle is a single thing in the strongest sense, and therefore individuality is an analogue of it.

No Distinction of Parts: The wholeness or singleness component of individuality is analogous to the property of a particle of having no distinction of parts within it.

Body: A particle has size and shape. If it did not, it would be a mere point, which would not distinguish it from empty space. But it has other properties as well as size and shape, since, if it had only size and shape it would, again, be a mere region of space and indistinguishable from empty space. Indeed, it is the other properties that give it *real* size and shape. I will use the word "form" to comprise all these properties. And these are the properties of the *body* of the particle — the particle without its relations with other entities. Then, the analogue of the body and its form is the property of things in general to have wholeness of form, which is analogous to the strict singleness of the body and form of a particle.

Structural Complementation: This is the principle that a complete particle includes its relations with other entities. Other modes of complementation are analogues of Structural Complementation.

An interesting analogue is the relationship between protons and electrons in an atom. The contrast between the body of a particle and the empty space around it is analogous to the contrast between the dense nucleus of the atom, consisting primarily of protons, and the rarefied cloud of much lighter electrons. The implication is that the structure of atoms evolved in part because of its analogy to Structural Complementation.

The two aspects of Structural Complementation are Surrounding Relations and Correspondence. The first is just the fact that the structural relations of a particle extend in various directions. That property is analogous to a branched structure, which is a common occurrence biologically. The second is the fact that the structural relations of a particle correspond one-to-one with the bodies related to the particle. By analogy with this, protons and electrons in an atom have a strong tendency to be in one-to-one correspondence. The structure of an atom, with the factor of electric charge keeping the protons and electrons in correspondence, combines these two analogies.

Contrast: The necessary pattern is the contrast between the body of a particle and the empty space immediately surrounding it. Contrast in general is an obvious analogue of it. Contrast is ubiquitous in nature and in technology. Distinctiveness is contrast. Contrast is essential for perception.

IN THE CATEGORY OF STRUCTURE

Patterns	Analogues
Connectedness	proximity (tendency = gravitation)
Separation	distinctiveness
Permanence	repetitive patterns
	endurance of things, repetitiveness,
	inertia; structural stability
Finitude	concepts of finitude
Spatiality	importance of visual imagery

Connectedness is the property that all bodies are structurally related by the same space. Proximity is analogous to this (if we compare being closely connected with being remotely connected, the former is more like being connected absolutely than is the latter). This is the necessary pattern for gravitation. Gravitation is the tendency of a particle-process to adjust its direction so as to move closer to other particles (to reduce its average distance from other particles). In terms of causality by patterns, the similarity of the potentiality to Connectedness is the sum of the proximities of all other particles to the potentiality, weighted by the values of the particles as quantity of matter (how this relates to mass in physics is not clear to me). If you compare the alternative potentialities of a particle-process across the cross-section in front of the process, their similarities to Connectedness form a distribution according to the sum just mentioned. Other patterns are combined with Connectedness to give the potencies of these potentialities.

Thus, if a particle-process is between two bodies, one more massive than the other, it tends to veer towards the more massive one.

Separation: This pattern is the separation between any two particles, necessary for their discreteness. Its analogue is the distinctiveness of individual structures and processes. The resulting tendency affects particles as well as compound structures, that is, particles not only are perfectly distinct but also tend to be distinctive. This tendency leads to a variety of particle types, and it also affects the spacing between particles. To be separated by space is necessary, but leaves the distance completely open; the tendency to be distinctive, which affects both particles and larger structures, puts them at "comfortable" distances. Physics reveals that those distances are greater than one would expect.

Permanence: This pattern is the permanent existence of whatever exists (nothing ever ceases to exist). Its analogue is the repetition of phases in a process, first of all in the mere fact of the continuation of the same process, and then in the repetition of similar phases. This tendency is inertia — the inertia of motion and the inertia of states of a process, for example, the tendency of a habit to persist.

Finitude: Early conceptions of the world saw it as finite, by analogy with its actual finitude. The atomists' conception of an infinite universe was probably inspired by geometry rather than structure. It is difficult to imagine space as finite, but difficult to imagine structure as infinite.

Spatiality: The universe is made of space and the things in it. Of all the sensory modalities, vision is the one that most fully and clearly represents the spatial relations among things. We can say, then, that vision most fully and clearly represents the fundamental character of the universe. I think that is why science has always been strongly shaped by the visual modality. To understand is to "see".

IN THE CATEGORY OF CHANGE

Patterns	**Analogues**
Extension	growth laterally in temporal space
New Existence	novelty, variety, creativity; concept of creation of the world; Generosity
Occurring Event	vivacity; playfulness, humour, creativity
Changing Structure	individual processes
Elementary Time	concept of a sequence
Permanence	memory, concept of past events
Discreteness	phase-individuality
1.Atomicity	phase-wholeness
2.Separateness	phase-distinctiveness
Finitude	concepts of beginning and end of world

Extension: Change is growth in temporal space in the direction of time. But to our senses, which are sensitive only to the living present (the range of active tendencies), it does not look like growth. What looks like growth is growth laterally to the direction of time, the expansion of the cross section of a process.   Growth in the ordinary sense, then, is an analogue of the extension of a process or of the universe. This would therefore be a cause of the general tendency of complex individual processes to grow.

New Existence: At each moment of elementary time a new particle comes into existence. This is the necessary pattern New Existence. This pattern is the companion to Permanence.   While Permanence is the basis for the tendency to prolong repetitiveness in a process, New Existence is the basis for the tendency to break a repetitive pattern. In human experience, we see these two tendencies competing with each other. And the condition for their respective potencies is the same. The longer a repetitive pattern continues the stronger the tendency for it to continue becomes. But also the stronger the tendency to switch to some available novelty becomes. This is because a potentiality to break a repetitive pattern is more clearly defined and therefore more similar to New Existence the more clearly repetitive the existing process is.

Occurring Event: Each moment of elementary time has two phases, one in which active tendencies exist followed by one in which a new particle comes into existence. At any particular moment these two phases constitute an actually occurring event. The necessary pattern Occurring Event is the set of all occurring events from the beginning of time to the present. Events in the past, of course, are no longer occurring. Having occurred, an actual event is completed and cannot continue to occur. However, it is then an event that has actually occurred, and is retained by the creative factor as such.

This necessary pattern consists of a sequence of tendencies and creations, and the creations are not determined by the preceding tendencies. It could therefore be characterized as both creative and playful. It has analogues such as vivacity, playfulness, humour, and creativity. The physics of particle events is also an analogue of this necessary pattern.

Changing Structure: At each moment of elementary time the structure of the universe is augmented by one particle. This is also the pattern of an individual process except that it would not gain a new particle at each moment of **elementary** time but at each moment of **local** time. Therefore, an individual process is an analogue of Changing Structure.

Elementary Time [47]: The concept of a sequence is an analogue of this necessary pattern, as are sequences in general. Permanence: This is the permanence of change, as distinct from the permanence of structure. The permanence of change consists in the fact that past changes have not gone out of existence but are still changes in the past. In other words, the past of elementary time exists; what exists is not merely the evanescent present. The important analogues of this necessary pattern are forms of the consciousness of the past, such as memory and the concept of past events.

Discreteness: There are minimal changes; each change has one unique successor. This property consists of two properties: the fact that no minimal change is composed of distinct changes (Atomicity); and the perfect separation of successive minimal changes (Separateness).

The analogues in individual processes in temporal space are phase-individuality (the tendency of a process to divide into distinctive phases with the property of wholeness), phase-distinctiveness, and phase-wholeness.

Finitude: At each moment of elementary time there have been only a finite number of changes. The concepts of a beginning of the world and also of the end of the world are analogues of this necessary pattern.

---

[47]See "The Dimensions of Time".

IN THE CATEGORY OF TENDENCY

<u>Patterns</u>	<u>Analogues</u>
Occurring Tendencies	the narrative arts & music
Origination	creativity, inspiration
Effective Pattern	modes of begetting: repetition in a process, biological reproduction, design & production, intention & action, influence of personal example
Potentially Effective Pattern	modes of potential begetting: fertilization, suggestion of ideas
Dynamic Complementation	dynamic sharing and relations: functional complementation, chemical bonding, public property, lovers' tokens, money, etc.

Occurring Tendencies: At each moment of elementary time there is a set of active tendencies. As moment succeeds moment, the active tendencies undergo changes consequent upon the creation of new particles. In human life, the progression of passions and emotions is an instance of Occurring Tendencies. The live arts are creative representations of that succession, therefore analogous to this necessary pattern. The significance of this analogy is that the necessary pattern combines with its human instances to heighten the potency of the artist's creative potentialities and to heighten the intensity of the experience of enjoying the live arts.

Origination: The extensions of the universe are never exactly like any combination of given patterns. As instances of necessary patterns they are exactly like all other instances, but not exactly like any other concrete entity. Each extension is an original creation, if only because of each new particle being in a new spatial relation with the others. Creativity and inspiration are analogues of this necessary pattern.

Effective Pattern & Potentially Effective Pattern: The analogy between a pattern that contributes to the realization of a potentiality similar to it and the begetting of offspring is obvious. The analogy between the begetting of offspring and the other analogues listed, I think, needs no explanation. And the importance of these analogies in biological life is obvious.

Dynamic Complementation: This pattern consists of the relational tendencies that exist between all adjacent processes in temporal space, also between all nested processes (related as whole and part). Emotional relations between persons are instances of this pattern. The analogues are relationships of a functional or emotional character. The implication, for example, is that the exchange of lovers' tokens is more poignant and the love of money more compulsive because of analogy to this necessary pattern.

An analogue calling for explanation is chemical bonding. I have suggested that electric charge and the structure of atoms are analogues of Structural Complementation. In standard physical chemistry, valence is due to the outer orbit of electrons having either fewer or more than the complete number of electrons, the noble gasses having complete outer orbits. In the present account the noble gasses have a higher level of wholeness than other elements because of their outer orbits being complete. The pattern of an atom (other than a noble gas), combined with the necessary patterns Particle and Discreteness and their analogue individuality has two contrary tendencies — to make the number of electrons equal to the number of protons (for the individuality of the atom), and to make the outer orbit of electrons complete and no more than complete (for the individuality of the outer orbit, as in the noble gasses). This can be practically accomplished in combination with another atom. If an ion (with either more or fewer than that number) is in proximity to another ion of the opposite kind (an excess combining with a deficit), there are one or more loose electrons which tend on the one hand to belong to the atom with the deficit to make up its outer orbit, and on the other hand to belong to the atom with the excess to make up its total number (equal to the number of protons). These two tendencies add up to a tendency for the atoms to remain in close proximity (to combine as a molecule). The shared electron may oscillate between the two atoms or stay in a stable position. So that is the account of chemical bonding that is implied by causality by patterns.

IN THE CATEGORY OF POTENTIAL EXTENSIONS

Patterns	**Analogues**
Supersession	succession of phases of a process, modes of sacrifice; predation, consumption of food, death & birth, self-sacrifice
Active Potentialities	functionality
Selection	competition; logical disjunction; choice; wholeness of functionality
1. Realization	an actual function; assertion, truth
2. Nullification	a counter-function; denial, falsity
3. Modification	a non-functional connecting process; suspending judgment, undecided statement
Continuity	concept of continuous matter & change
Unboundedness	concept of unending future & unbounded space
Possibility	concepts of future possibilities, options; non-existent things
Potentiality as Tendency	concepts of probable future events, causal efficacy, tendency, & force

Supersession: This is the succession of active tendencies. At each new moment of elementary time a new set of potentialities and active tendencies supersedes the preceding set. This succession is what we experience as the passage of time; it is the experience of changing tendencies.

The succession of distinctive phases of a process is an analogue. But more important from a human perspective are the various forms of sacrifice — the old generation giving way to the new generation, life being destroyed to feed other life, the older generation foregoing pleasures to care for the younger generation, and so on.

Active Potentialities: At every moment of elementary time a new set of active potentialities occurs. Functionality is the property of a system of tending to support and/or create individuality. Active potentialities tend to result in particles, which are analogous to individuality. Thus, the necessary pattern Active Potentialities has functionality as an analogue.

Selection: This pattern is the selection of a potentiality for realization at each moment of elementary time. Competition and choice are obvious analogues. Logical disjunction is an analogue because some potentialities are selected and the remainder are not.

A function is a process in temporal space that contributes to the individuality of one or more processes. Wholeness of functionality is the condition of a functional system where the functional parts work together consistently to further the same individualities, rather than working against one another. In the real world of living beings, there are always counter-functional processes arising through opportunistic individuality, so that defences against these counter-functions (counter-functions to the counter-functions) are needed in order to achieve wholeness of functionality.

To see why wholeness of functionality is an analogue of Selection, we have to consider its sub-patterns and their analogues. Realization is the realization of certain potentialities when a new particle is created. Nullification is the occupation of the space where the nullified potentiality might have been realized, by the realization of other potentialities. Nullification eliminates a potentiality, and a potentiality is analogous to a function, so nullification is analogous to opposing some individuality, therefore analogous to a counter-function. Now, the realized potentialities are analogous to actual or successful functions, because they have actually become extended processes. Therefore, when the creative factor selects a potentiality, the realization of that one nullifies another, which would have nullified it (the function eliminates the counter-function). So this is analogous to a condition where the decent people oppose the criminals, the counter-functions are opposed by the functions, resulting in wholeness of functionality.

The remaining analogues of Realization, Nullification, and Modification are at the foundation of the communication of information. The realization of a potentiality gives it actuality, just as asserting a statement attributes actuality to what it represents. And the truth of an affirmative statement is equivalent to the actuality of what it represents. Correspondingly, the nullification of a potentiality denies it actuality, just as asserting the denial of a statement denies actuality to what it represents. And the falsity of a statement is equivalent to the non-actuality of what it represents. Then the analogues of Modification correspond to these.

Continuity, Unboundedness, Possibility, & Potentiality as Tendency: These are some of those concepts that have proven difficult to analyse and yet are quite intuitive. Their rootedness in a necessary pattern helps to explain how this is possible.

IN THE CATEGORY OF TRANSCENDENCE

<u>Pattern</u>	<u>Analogue</u>
Creation	generosity, procreation, vivacity, concept of God
Truth, or responding to things exactly as they are	truth, truthfulness, responsibility
Rootedness (soul)	concept of a soul
Influence (spirit)	concept of spirit; procreation

Creation: the creation of a particle at each moment of elementary time.   I think the analogues are obvious enough.

Truth: the creative factor's inability to sense things otherwise than exactly as they are.   Again, the analogues are obvious.

Rootedness: Each thing is related by similarity to things in the past (or present) and to all things by its analogues to the necessary patterns.   In the case of a living individual, its rootedness constitutes its soul.   Therefore, the concept of a soul is an analogue of the necessary pattern.

Influence: Each thing is a pattern for its own potentialities and for the potentialities of other similar things.   In the case of a living individual, its influence is its spirit, so that the concept of spirit is an analogue.   Procreation is also an analogue, since in causality by patterns the pattern gives rise to similar entities or phases.

The first two of these patterns are relationships of an entity in temporal space **with** the creative factor, while the last two are relationships **through** the creative factor.   But a relationship **through** the creative factor is first a relationship **with** the creative factor, and then with the third relatum (a pattern or a potentiality).   Therefore, if we understand God to be the creative factor in its relationships with things in temporal space, then God is defined by these four necessary patterns, but primarily by the first three.

ALTERNATION OF SPATIAL & STRUCTURAL EXTENSION

Pattern (two phases)	Analogue or Tendency
Spatial-to-Structural-to-Spatial (alarm)	
1.Spatial Extension	loss of individuality
2. Structural Extension	attempt to regain individuality
Structural-to-Spatial-to-Structural (elation)	
1. Structural Extension	gain of individuality
2. Consequent Spatial Extension	gain of individuality seizing opportunity

These necessary patterns are part of the foundation of basic emotions due to gains or losses of individuality.

There are two necessary patterns here, each with two phases. At each moment of elementary time there is a state in which the structure of the universe and each individual process has a spatial extension that defines a set of potentialities, and the comparison of these with patterns defines a set of tendencies. Then on that basis, the creative factor creates a particle to occupy the space in front of the structure. And the consequence of this is another state with another set of potentialities and tendencies. There is an alternation, then, between spatial extensions and structural extensions.

The analogy that makes these patterns relevant to emotions is this, that space is not individuated whereas structure is, so that the transition from a spatial extension to a structural extension is analogous to a gain of individuality, while the transition from a structural extension to a spatial extension is analogous to a loss of individuality.

The tendency to maximize individuality determines the response in either case. Given a loss of individuality, one seeks to regain it, and given a gain of individuality, one seeks to take advantage of those circumstances for a further gain. So there is a cause phase and an effect phase. Then those phases match one or other of these necessary patterns, so that the circumstances of a gain or loss, the necessary patterns Particle and Discreteness, and the necessary pattern Alternation of Spatial and Structural Extension all combine compatibly, giving wholeness of similarity, to intensify the tendency and the emotion.

EFFECTS OF CHANGE ON POTENTIALITIES

Pattern	Analogue, Tendency, Emotion
Realized	opportunity taken, capability demonstrated, success foreseen; complacency or self-confidence
Modified Unchanged	opportunity or capability constant; response unchanged
Modified Up	opportunity or capability improved; exhilaration, seizing opportunity
Modified Down	opportunity or capability worsened; depression, neglect of opportunity
Nullified	opportunity or capability lost; downcast, at a loss

The necessary patterns here are the different changes in the potencies of potentialities resulting from events. Potentialities are analogous to opportunities presented by circumstances; indeed, opportunities **are** the potentialities of circumstances. Potentialities are also analogous to capabilities; indeed, capabilities **are** potentialities of the state of a person. This group of necessary patterns and analogues is parallel to the previous group. Those in the previous group are analogous to **actual** gains and losses of individuality, while these are analogous to **potential** gains and losses of individuality. Potential gains and losses of individuality have the same emotional impact as actual gains and losses, except that the impact is usually less intense.

COMPARATIVE POTENCIES

Pattern	Analogue, Tendency, Emotion
Potency High (realized)	superior opportunity or capability; enthusiasm or complacency, seizing opportunity; self-concept as superior or lucky
Potency Low (unrealized)	inferior opportunity or capability; depression, anger; neglect of opportunity or greater effort; self-concept as inferior or unlucky

In the universe, potentialities in the past are partitioned into the two classes of realized and unrealized potentialities. Potentialities with higher potencies are more likely to be realized, so that statistically the realized potentialities had higher potencies than the unrealized. Potentialities are realized in the creation of particles, and individuality is an analogue of particles. These two necessary patterns are behind the emotions due to comparing one's own potentialities (opportunities, capabilities, circumstances) with those of others or of another.[48] Superior opportunity is opportunity for higher levels of individuality, and similarly for inferior. Therefore, superior opportunity or capability is analogous to higher potency and inferior opportunity or capability is analogous to lower potency.

---

[48]See "Emotion & Feeling" in "Consciousness, Choice, & Reasoning".

ABOUT THE AUTHOR

Will Crichton received his Ph.D. in Philosophy from The University of Michigan. He was a Professor in the Faculty of Philosophy at the University of Toronto teaching philosophy for many years. He was co-author of a translation of Rilke's *The Duino Elegies*. Born August 30, 1928 in Toronto, he died December 5, 2002 in Toronto.

INDEX

D